Without Me You'll Be Eating Out of Garbage Cans

by
Lori Wilk

Writers Club Press
San Jose · New York · Lincoln · Shanghai

To Craig, Bill, Tracy, Mom, Dad, Grandpa Sol and Rosalie.
In loving memory of Alice and Harry Krieger, Helen Horowitz,
Vickie Greene and Fenway.

Acknowledgements:

Special thanks to The Writer's Club for making this on-line, on-demand publishing possible and for all the help publishing this book. Shirley Bryant, you're great. And thanks to Milk Altman at iUniverse.com for his help with the final editing.

Thanks to Frank, Jennifer, Matt , Alexis, B.J., Alice, Tiku, Margo and Kristi for all the emotional support and encouragement.

CONTENTS

Introduction

Hi there! I'm glad the title of my book got your attention. At least you were curious about someone being told that by breaking up with someone else, they would experience the worst imaginable fate: being so broke they would be eating out of garbage cans.

Well don't worry too much about me eating out of garbage cans. I was the real estate investment specialist who helped this man get rich. As a thank-you for my efforts, he threw me out of the home I found, negotiated the deal on, and helped remodel, on the day I completed my MBA.

As I pulled into the driveway he said, "If you're leaving, you might as well go now and you know, without me, you'll be eating out of garbage cans."

His words shattered my nerves. I couldn't believe it was happening to me. How dare he think that I had no value; that I couldn't make a living without him. He had millions because my education and expertise enabled me to select investments for him which made him rich.

I could have been one of the first women in Florida to file a palimony lawsuit, which might have forced him to share the money with me, but I knew he would fight me to the end and with his temper and track record I didn't want to take the chance of getting killed or seriously injured. I still had my son to raise, so I considered an alternative: moving on.

I had to start over again and find a new path. In this breakup I lost my business, the roof over my head, my cash flow and my emotional well being. Healing emotionally was a challenge because I couldn't erase from my mind how hard I worked for four and a half years and I was shocked he could throw me out like garbage.

Yes. I felt drained, like there was nothing left. Then one day, I realized that there was something left: a gift. The horrible words, which tore me apart, were really a gift I could share . His words were the motivation I needed to write this book and now I've made them the title, too!

This book is about realizing that it doesn't matter how educated you are or what your financial status is, you can be involved in a relationship which is mentally, physically or emotionally abusive, a relationship you might be better off without.

In this book, I share my own experiences and ideas plus those of others who have been abused . The names have all been changed to protect the identity of all parties involved.

To eliminate abuses, we must know they exist, acknowledge them and not deny them. We must overcome our fears, know we have value, believe in ourselves and our right to desire a better life. We must take steps to make this happen.

This book was self-published to get the information out quickly without asking for anyone's permission to write the story or their money to pay for it. I was emotionally devastated and it took about five years to recover. Laughing helped, writing this book helped ;talking about abuse to national audiences on radio and television is next.

I am here for you because I can't be there. I hope you enjoy my book and that my words give you strength, power , emotional support and encouragement for the road ahead . I'm looking forward to meeting many of you soon.

1

NOW, WOULD BE FINE

Patience is for those who are willing to wait.

-Lori Wilk

Now, Would Be Fine

Since yesterday is gone and I don't know what tomorrow will bring, I have to conclude that now is the time to do this work.

When I told my mother I was writing a book about abuse, to let other women know that they should not tolerate any form of abuse, she was surprised and couldn't understand why I selected this topic. She suggested I write about something else. I procrastinated about writing this book , then decided to write it anyway.

Write about something else? According to what I have learned, if you have something to say, you should say it. There are people who need to hear what you are saying.

In the book, "Live Your Dreams," by Motivational Author and Speaker, Les Brown, "When you are trying to decide what to do about your dreams, you should ask yourself the questions: If I don't do this work, who will and if not now, when ?" As you will read in my chapter ,Wake-Up Calls, I have learned that time waits for no one.

Les Brown also wrote about a woman who had ideas for some fabulous creative projects. She died unexpectedly without ever seeing her projects created. Waiting and ignoring my desire to share my experiences and ideas with anyone who needs them was not an option. Besides, if I didn't write about abuse, it wouldn't just go away.

I knew I was not suffering alone from emotional abuse. There are many women out there who feel alone, scared, confused or just plain sick and tired of being abused in any way. Many women don't know where to begin to get out of their situations or how they can go about making their lives better.

It's a fact that gravity keeps us attached to this planet, but what force keeps us in relationships or situations which are mentally, physically or emotionally abusive? I will write about some of these reasons in this book. Far too many women, the number of them is staggering: nationally approximately 4 million women a year are victims of domestic abuse. Even one is too many. Especially if the one being abused is you.

As a result of all this abuse, more than 100,000 women are hospitalized and more than 2,000 will die. Many more millions of women are victims of mental and/or emotional abuses, but their numbers are harder to quantify. They often suffer silently for years, their pain not readily noticed, their stories never told.

The fact remains that even when the door is in sight, many, who should go, don't use it as an exit. Too many woman stay in abusive situations and for some of them, sadly, until it's too late.

Now is the time to talk, to find answers, to help others and to finally take action. If I can help even one person with this book. It will be worth all of the time it took to write it and all of the money spent to publish it.

2

WAKE-UP CALLS

Life is not like a VCR.
We can't put our lives on hold.
There is no pause or reverse button.
You can't push rewind to start over.
No matter what you missed.

-Lori Wilk

If God does in fact send us messages from above, then I was notified with a series of wake-up calls to publish this book.

First call: The death of my paternal Grandmother, Helen Horowitz.

Grandma Helen could have written this book, using her life as the example of an unbelievable tolerance of long-term abuse. Her abusive marriage lasted more than 50 years .She was still married at the time of her death, but not happily.

Grandma Helen was an incredibly talented homemaker who made beautiful crafts. She handmade most of the clothing my sister and I wore when we were growing up, she was an excellent cook , she was great at crossword puzzles, loved to knit and crochet and was an avid reader.

The only thing holding her back was her poor hearing. My mom felt that Grandma lacked the self-confidence she would have needed to support herself if she asked for a divorce because of her hearing. I used to think that God protected Grandma by making it so she couldn't hear all the bad things Grandpa used to say to her all those years.

My memories of Grandpa's verbal and emotional abuse were that not only did his behavior destroy Grandma, it upset my mother . Every time my grandparents came to visit, my mother would lock herself in the bathroom and cry.

I have been told that Grandpa was verbally abused by his father during his childhood. He was put down and his self-esteem destroyed. Children who are emotionally abused often grow up in a state of depression and don't get rid of this depression or feeling of unworthiness as adults unless they get professional help. Abuse, I am told ,continues on to the next generation unless the cycle of abuse is stopped.

Grandpa Sol took advantage of the fact that Grandma Helen didn't hear very well . He said negative things about her. In their later years when I visited them, four letter words were common in their conversations. I felt more like a referee at a boxing match than like a grandchild visiting her grandparents. He battered her verbally in one breath and claimed he couldn't live without her in next. She was more like a habit he couldn't break than a wife.

In the late 1980's , Grandma called me, desperate for help. She asked me to take her to a lawyer for a divorce. The lawyer told her to forget about a divorce because he couldn'timagine any judge throwing an 80-yr.-old man out of his home. The lawyer told her to hang in there. Disappointed, she checked out mentally, emotionally and then physically.

Grandma was humiliated by some of grandpa's actions over the years. He often acted more like 18 than 80, although that could explain why he still alive at almost 90. He was arrested for propositioning a woman while in his 70's . Unfortunately, he didn't have fun because she was an undercover officer. He lost his home healthcare worker for inappropriate requests during bathtime and was asked to move from the nursing home where he lived briefly before Grandma died.

In the last few years of her life, she was so depressed and upset that she wanted to end her life. She tried to commit suicide several times by overdosing on her medications. She completely stopped all her creative activities. No more cooking, no more sewing, no more knitting, no nothing. She stayed in her chair all day and refused to move. Eventually, her system shut down and she died.

It's not easy writing about family and the imperfections. Writing about grandpa as being abusive will probably make some family members angry, but I'll take my chances and speak the truth , because that's all that's left . Ignoring the truth won't make it go away or bring Grandma back.

This was the first call. More calls came soon after grandma passed on. One night I woke up at 2am to take my dog for a walk . I had to go through the den to get to the kitchen for a glass of water. The house was dark and quiet, until I entered the den. All of a sudden, the television set turned on, by itself.

I was amazed and startled, but not knowing what to do, I just stared at the television. Then, as I stared, it started to change channels by itself. I screamed for my boyfriend and he came running to my rescue.

As we both watched the television in amazement, the volume got louder and louder and then the next thing that crossed my mind was Grandma Helen. Grandma, with her hearing loss , always had to put the volume on the television up really loud to hear it. We didn't know what to do next, so we shut off the television and went back to bed.

A few days later, I came home after dark, once again to a quiet home with no lights on and again, as I entered the den, the television turned on, all by itself . This bothered me, but I didn't know what to do, so I unplugged the television and removed it from the den and it is still sitting in another room, unplugged.

Were the strange happenings with the television a sign of a visitation from my Grandmother or just something else unrelated?

I don't know, but I'd like to think that Grandma is happy about my writing this book.

The next call caught me off guard. It was a Saturday morning and I was headed out the door to the local yard sales to search for antiques and collectibles. I said good-bye to Trouble, the puppy that lived outside on my back porch.

A few hours later I returned to the house to get something and expected to be greeted at my car door by Trouble. He wasn't there. I considered this odd, but figured he went for a walk somewhere on our 3 acres property.

I left for a few more hours and then returned home. Once again, Trouble was not there to greet me. At that point, I figured out that Trouble was in some sort of trouble of his own. A message on my answering machine confirmed my fears: A medium sized brown dog had been hit by a truck and killed. Trouble was gone.

He just wanted to cross the highway to have some fun with the dogs on the other side. He didn't know that the speed limit on the road was 55 mph and that most drivers are in such a hurry that they're traveling at closer to 70 mph .

It was then that I realized that this puppy left me with a message, that time is an issue and that you never know how much time you have during this lifetime to do what you're supposed to do, so you can't waste any precious time.

"Hello. This is God speaking, I have a collect, person-to-person call for Lori Wilk. Is she available? I'd like to speak to her as soon as possible, " he said. .." What do you mean she is too busy to take my calls?" he asked.

Thanksgiving was rapidly approaching. There was so much to be thankful for. I was looking forward to getting together with my family in Atlanta and had even requested a few days off from my job so that I'd have enough time to drive. I came down with a flu and couldn't go.

My Step-Mother has lymes disease. Her immune system was weakened by antibiotics which were used to try to kill the disease. I couldn't bring flu germs which she might not be able to fight off.

My dad called on Thanksgiving. He never calls me, unless there is a problem, or he wants me to do something for him. He doesn't call just to say "Hello." I love him, but, dread his phone calls because they don't bring good news.

This was a problem call. While my Step-Mom was watching television, waiting for the turkey to be done, she had a stroke and was rushed to the hospital. Within 48 hours she had a series of eight strokes and was a totally different person than the one I knew.

Time. It hit me in the face this round. Time is very important. I couldn't keep missing Gods calls. There was something I needed to do, immediately.

The next call came at Christmas. This time the connection was a little clearer. The caller informed me that my father had been so stressed from caring for his wife and elderly father that he sort of blew his cork. He had a brain hemorrhage. I was told to get in my car and drive to Atlanta.

In a matter of moments, this brain hemorrhage sent him from a vibrant businessman to a mess. Time was a really important and not wasting it, even more important. The volume on the phone calls was getting louder and the message more clear. It was as if Grandma was turning up the sound from Heaven.

Although I don't know where the messages are coming from., they've gotten to me that it is time for me to speak, write, publish and share this information with the world . It's a big job, but at least I'm getting started. I do have a question:" If I have to do all this work, will you send me a few helpers or guides and a few more clues?"

The line was busy. Maybe my answers will come soon.

Another call came during the editing phase of this book. It was a Friday night. I promised to take my son, Craig, ice-skating. Before pulling out of the driveway, I stopped to yell at Craig because he was not being appreciative of anything. His attitude was very negative and this was upsetting me. I finished yelling and then pulled out of the driveway to take him to the skating rink.

As I drove down the road I tried to explain why I was upset. I tried to get him to understand that he had so much to be thankful for. We were only about a mile from our home when he arrived at the scene of an overturned vehicle.

I stopped, pulled to the side of the road and we both jumped out of the car and ran towards the overturned vehicle to see if there were people trapped inside who needed help.

Craig was running in front of me and was getting to the crash faster since I was wearing high heels and a dress. Before making it to the overturned vehicle, he saw a young child who had apparently been thrown to the pavement from the impact of this crash and had lost his life.

A police officer arrived at the scene and my son claims he covered the young child's body with a brand new Tommy Hilfiger shirt. Designer clothing took on a new meaning. Labels were not important in life. Life was more important than the labels.

Inside the overturned vehicle a woman and her teen-aged son were trapped, in need of medical attention and the Jaws of Life to get them out from between the crushed metal. The best I could do was provide emotional support and pray that help would arrive quickly. I got down on the ground, talked to them while they were upside down and tried to keep them calm, while reassuring them that help was on the way.

I heard another child crying on the opposite side of the vehicle and I heard other people helping, so I stayed with the mom and son who were trapped upside down.

What do you talk about in a situation like this?

I asked about their day, where they were coming from and what they were doing before the accident happened. The mom said they had been fishing and shopping and were on the way home after a fun day.

Finally, the police, fire and rescue arrived at the scene. There was nothing more I could do, so I continued driving to the skating rink. When I got out of the car I realized that I was bleeding from cuts on my leg and arm which came lying on the ground on broken glass at the crash site while talking to the mom and her son. I didn't feel the cuts when I got them, but they were a painful reminder of the accident for a few weeks after.

I saved the newspaper article about the crash and was reminded of the fatality by a wreath which they placed at the crash site. I never got up the nerve to call the mom or to find out if the second child who had been thrown through the window lived, but I have thought about them many times and wondered why we were placed at the scene at that time.

Had I not stopped in my driveway to yell at my son, I would have been at the accident site sooner and we may have witnessed the accident happening or been involved in the wreck. Something made me stop in the driveway, delaying our arrival at the accident scene.

I have thanked God for not getting us there sooner to witness this horrible event or to have been involved in it in any other way.

My plan was to teach my son a lesson and God showed us a fatality, more than I ever would have imagined. According to the accounts I have heard of this accident, one child died, the second was listed in critical condition upon arrival at the hospital from the injuries due to the impact of being thrown through the windshield on to the pavement. These children were not wearing their seatbelts.

The mother and son trapped inside the vehicle had their seatbelts on. I was told that the driver, the mom, was at fault in this accident because she was being impatient. Witnesses to the accident said she tried to pass another vehicle by going around it. She was going more than 55mph when she drove off the concrete road to the grass to pass the car in front of her and her vehicle flipped when she drove back on to the concrete, causing this tragedy.

In a matter of seconds the mom's life had changed forever. I had some scars from the cuts which kept the incident fresh in my mind for a while, but the mom has emotional scars which will probably last her lifetime.

Time... the message came again, should not be wasted or taken for granted. No more calls, please. I know it's time to do this work.

I had gotten the message, when another unexpected call came with news I was told I would not like. My Yorkie, Fenway, had ventured off the property and was killed by a car. My son saw him lying in the street. This was more than I could take.

Fenway, my loyal little friend for almost 7 years, was gone. This was my final wake-up call before I published this book and it represented the time I knew that the writing and editing phases of book publishing were over. It signaled the time to plant seeds for the new growth phase: promotion and selling of this book and sharing its messages with the audience and readers.

To symbolize this new phase of work, we planted Wild-flower seeds on Fenways grave and will look forward to seeing the results of this work blossom.

I now believe that we are continually being given clues about how to proceed with our lives but that we often ignore these messages until a crisis takes place. Our lives are so busy that we often concentrate on everything else but the source of our problems and pains. Maybe it's time to start tuning in to some of these signals and messages instead of pushing them aside.

As far as the message goes, I didn't personally "get it" right the first time, second time or even the third. Yes, I admit to having screwed up more than once and I hope you won't wait that long or make the same mistakes.

The purpose of this book is to open lines of communication, to get you thinking about your own personal reality and to make you honest with yourself. If while being honest with yourself, you consider making a change in your life, I hope you do it now, or at least before it's too late. Change is about making choices and no matter how bad things get you still have choices and decisions to make. Remember, doing nothing is also a choice.

3

ROLE MODELS

When my parents divorced, almost 23 years ago, mom re-entered the job market with a High School Diploma and almost 20 years experience as a homemaker. She struggled to find a good paying job. I learned from her experiences that education and credentials are essential.

I promised myself to never let a man stand in the way of my getting an education. I have to admit, they tried. To a man, a smart woman who can take care of herself financially can be intimidating, harder to control, and to that I say, "intimidate them anyway and get educated. He might be gone tomorrow, but your education will stay with you forever. Getting more education enhances your self-esteem , builds up your confidence and makes you more marketable in the business world."

My sister and I grew up in the shadows of mom's emotional pain and denial. There's no time left for denial . I have now turned the pain into a tool.

A crisis often brings change. Mom reached a point where the pain of staying in the marriage was greater than the pain that would be caused by leaving. The death of her mother, Alice Krieger, from Cancer, brought her to that turning point.

Before leaving us, Grandma Alice taught us some very valuable lessons about speaking up and honesty, although we didn't see her actions as lessons at the time.

Grandma Alice had Cancer of the bone marrow . It began somewhere in her head and worked its way down her spine. Her spine collapsed, the Cancer destroyed her body and did bizarre things to her mind. She was often in excruciating pain, but her incredible personality prevailed until the end.

While Grandma Alice was living in our two-story brick home in Brooklyn, New York, where she and Grandpa Harry lived downstairs and we lived upstairs, she experienced telephone seizures in which her mind went off track.

During these telephone seizures, she made continuous phone calls and had non-stop conversations both real and imaginary. The topic of the conversation was whatever was on her mind and nothing mattered other than that she had to keep talking and holding on to the telephone.

Who did she call? Stockbrokers, politicians, friends, family, strangers.... lots of people. She purchased stocks, told people what she thought of them and she decided to run for Mayor. Grandma Alice asked me to run her campaign. She believed in me.

In the phase of her disease, when she was suffering the most, she was also the most honest with people. I don't know if she knew her time was limited, but she held nothing back. She said things which shocked people because she was so blunt and in retrospect, some of the comments were really funny..

It was difficult losing my favorite person in the world at 14, but her actions taught me that you shouldn't wait until you are dying to start living the life you want, don't push your feelings aside, and don't tolerate abuse. Take action to make changes if things or people are not right for you . The sooner the better.

4

DOUBLE TROUBLE

Relationships don't always start out bad. In many cases, they get bad over time.I found out that I met the man who changed my life three years before we were officially introduced. This lead me to question whether our meeting was destined to happen or if meeting him and learning important lessons were inevitable.

While operating a real estate brokerage, I hired a Sales Associate who had been reading a book about the future which explained that property near the ocean had long-term growth potential and he advised me to consider buying property in South Beach in Miami Beach, Florida.

South Beach had so much distressed real estate available. I went with him to South Beach to look at a few properties and searched the newspapers for deals. I loved the Art Deco Architecture and could see all sorts of possibilities with some pastel colored paint and new carpet.

My next challenge was to find a property which could be purchased for little or no money down, because whatever cash I had would be needed for the repairs. I found a deal on a 34-unit building which was fully occupied.

The nightmares began the morning after the closing when my full building was half empty. The tenants who were not paying moved out after the closing. I considered re-selling the property once I found out its true condition and income status and placed an ad in the newspaper to find a buyer.

The man who changed my life forever answered the ad. He said that if I wanted to get out from underneath the property, I should give him the deed. I told him he was crazy and he drove off, only to resurface three years later by formal introduction.

Our introduction, and the second time he crossed my path, although I didn't realize this at the time, came as the result of a call from a Realtor friend who said he had a client he thought might be good for me, a very good referral.

This client was an investor who wanted to buy distressed properties and he thought that I would be the best person to help him since distressed properties for investors was not his specialty. I thanked him for the referral and agreed to meet the client.

When we were introduced, this client made me an offer I didn't want to refuse. He offered to provide me with the tools I needed to buy as much distressed property as I could find which fit his investment criteria. He seemed to believe in me and that got my attention.

I saw our meeting as an opportunity and agreed to help him acquire properties.

5

THE SIGNS WERE POSTED

If you're like most people, you've probably had at least one relationship which didn't turn out the way you expected. In fact, there may have been clues along the way to let you know that something was wrong, but you might have ignored them. Sometimes, we are so close to a situation that we can't see it clearly. That's why other people tend to notice we're in a bad relationship before we do.

Maybe we don't want to get hurt. Maybe we don't want to lose what we have for fear that we won't be able to replace it with anything better. Maybe we just are hoping it will get better with time and deep down inside, we might really want things to work out. We don't want to feel that our relationships, our lives or anything we are a part of is not unsuccessful. It's not good for our self-esteem.

As a mom with a 2-year-old son to support, I had the blinders on and was focusing only on earning a good living, taking care of my son and on furthering my education. I truly believed I was in a relationship. I ignored some of the things that today seem very strange.

Once I had generated a substantial number of business deals, I asked him for a commitment. I wanted to know that there would be some sort of security for myself and my son. He gave me a three and a half carat diamond ring. This made me believe that the money I was making was ultimately for all of us to enjoy. I had no idea he intended the money to be for himself.

Being a woman, I made the error of thinking like one too. There was no contract to back me up and no long-term benefits derived from having this "commitment" from him without a legal battle.

There were signs posted to give me clues that I was not in a loving relationship, but I wasn't paying attention or reading the signs.

First there were his hang-ups: He didn't want me to sleep in his bedroom because he didn't want me to take up his air . He yelled shut-up every time I sneezed, which was often due to my allergies and sinus problems.

I met one of his former girlfriends and she said he broke her nose one day. I figured accidents happen. Then a co-worker told me that another of his previous girlfriends was killed by the jealous husband of a woman he was having an alleged affair with. This was too much to consider so I didn't ask any more questions.

When we discussed real estate and my interest in additional education, he didn't like the idea and was not supportive. " Why do you want to know how to build houses when you can steal equity?, " he asked.

During our time together we lived in 12 different homes, fixed them up and sold them. The first property I helped him remodel was the penthouse where he was living when we met. It had lots of square footage but the decor was outdated. I recommended he remove the heavy drapes, take the flocked wallpaper off the bathroom walls, remove the old shag carpet, eliminate the brown vinyl kitchen floor , paint the walls white, add mirrors to the bathroom and closet doors, lay new beige plush carpet , install bright white lights in the kitchen and raise the price of the condo $100,000. It sold almost immediately.

I didn't walk away from this relationship even after having received death threats from a disgruntled buyer who lost money in a transaction with him. I stayed although I witnessed a fight with a tenant who threatened to destroy his property and was taken on a high speed chase to catch this tenant once he did $30,000 worth of damage to one of his homes. I even checked into a hotel several times to avoid being at home when I thought tenants were after him.

The bottom line is that we don't believe the signs until they smack us in the face and we have to deal with the reality. When there's almost no other choice, we change.

6

DON'T YOU WANT ME BABY?

I was intrigued and attracted to real estate at the age of 18. I was introduced to real estate by a man considerably older than myself. He drove an expensive car and told me about investing in real estate and making hundreds and thousands of dollars.

He shared stories with me about buying property in Miami's Coconut Grove section of town, pre-construction and by merely putting a downpayment on these condos in the pre-construction phase...before they were built... and waiting until they were ready and finding a buyer for them while they were under construction, he was getting rich.

I was hooked. Real estate go my attention . I could make money and it was very exciting. We went out together dancing to the fancy Coconut Grove discos. He wore plenty of gold jewelry and had a car phone before most people and an attitude to match.

After going out for a while, he wanted to show me this new Coconut Grove condo. It had just been completed. It was on a high floor with an incredible bay view. He was one of the first residents in the building to have moved in. Everything seemed innocent, until I got to his apartment.

I realized that what seemed so beautiful could turn ugly on me and that I was in a situation I didn't want to be in. The building was mostly unoccupied. That meant, we were really alone.

The condo was on a very high floor, so I wasn't jumping off the balcony and I was a young girl with a man who was interested in me, not showing me the condo.

This was the 70's. People liked disco and going out . Here I was in a fancy building with the security guard far away and I was overcome with this weird feeling that I should get out of there. The feeling got stronger as he tried to make moves on me.

The large bed, the fur skinned rugs, the stereo system to drown out any sound that I could possibly make was making me very uncomfortable. He wanted me and I did not want him. He left me alone for a few minutes, I think he went into the bathroom and I took the opportunity to call my mother to come pick me up and to exit his condominium.

This was not the last time I encountered strange men in expensive places in Miami, but it started teaching me that I had to be very careful and that having fun could turn out to be very dangerous.

Your upbringing does a lot to shape your beliefs. My parents gave me the impression that I should look for a successful man who was making good money. Someone who could be a good provider. My father was a businessman..

I found men with money, or maybe they found me, but too often, that was their only good point. The negatives outweighed the money. I even started to learn that money is not a good reason to be in a relationship, although there will be women who want to tell me I'm wrong and there's nothing like money.

Money is great and it helps you do many things, but the money I want nowadays is the money I make myself. I will no longer trade money as a reason to tolerate abuse.

There was a professional photographer who had a kinkier side and liked to play. I liked to play too and dressed up and experimented with new things. Well, the night we went back to his condo in Coconut Grove, he decided to experience an altered state of mind by popping a few pills and I would not tolerate that. If you can't experience me in full reality, you can't be with me in something virtual, so I was leaving.

He didn't want me to go and that was understandable, I'm desirable, but since he had already taken the liberty of removing his clothes and yet was still following me to the elevator, the older couple who were inside when it opened were in for a little shock. He stood naked in front of the elevator and begged me to stay.

I am white, but I think my face was very red on the trip to the lobby. I didn't say a word to the older couple. I was not about to explain that scene.

During my last year of High School, I attended Miami-Dade Community College. I skipped the first year of college by exams and then completed my second year of college and earned a broadcasting degree, the same day I graduated from High School. I earned a debate scholarship and was a public speaker to earn money to pay for my education.

Part of my college program included studies in International Relations. I learned that men from other countries have different ideas about women and often treat them differently than American men do. In many countries it is very diffult for women to be executives, because men won't deal with them at all as decision makers.

While doing research for this book, I read about how abuse is handled in other countries. In Caracas, for example, I read that 8 out of 10 women who wind up in the emergency room, are there due to domestic violence. Legislation to protect women from abuse and to help them has taken the last seven years to pass. It is my understanding that during 1999 new laws will finally go into effect to help women who are abused in Venezuela. These laws include free trials , more shelters and more assistance programs.

In the UK, as of five years ago, there were approximately 100,000 women per year seeking treatment in London for violent injuries received in the home. And it was reported that more than 25% of all violent crime reported to police is domestic violence.

Although more than 30,000 women and children stay in refuge in the UK, there is not enough space to meet the demand. Here in the US, there are three times as many shelters for animals as there are humans.

According to the US Dept. of Justice, domestic violence is the leading cause of injury to women, more than muggings, stranger rape and car accidents combined.

On average, a women is beaten 9 times before she places the first call to police for help; only 7% of all spousal assaults are even reported to the police.

In fact, 57% of women who are physically abused by their partners never tell anyone. Approximately 50% of all homeless women and children are fleeing from domestic violence situations.

The American Bar Association information stated that evidence has shown that the danger of violence increases, including the risk of death, when a domestic violence survivor attempts to leave a batterer. They acknowledge that seeking legal assistance is seen as a step towards independence. The mere thought of a partner being able to leave threatens the batterer's sense of control and may further enrage the batterer, and that could endanger the abuse survivor. Get help to get away, professional help is often needed . Plans for your safety are critical.

Precautions are often necessary. According to more US Dept. Of Justice statistics, 79% of spousal abuse is committed by the men, after the woman leaves.

Pregnant women are at twice the risk of battery as non-pregnant women and the United Way ranks domestic violence as the leading cause of birth defects.

Not only are we endangered as victims of domestic, physical or emotional abuse, more than 3 million children a year will witness acts of domestic violence. All of these numbers make you realize that this is a huge problem and something has to be done.

There are thousands of websites with information about abuse including statistics, phone numbers where you can call for help, suggestions about what you can do, information about where you can go and even how to cover your tracks if you have a computer savvy spouse who is tracking your moves and research on the computer. I have a resource section at the end of the book.

7

GETTING AN EDUCATION

As I mentioned earlier, after my parents divorced, it was difficult for my mother to get a good paying job with only a High School education and twenty years of experience as a homemaker, but not current workplace experience. Luckily she had typing skills.

I was determined to get a good education and knew I'd be paying for it myself so I had to figure out what to do. I took the CLEP exams and passed in many subjects which enabled me to skip the first year of college and I was awarded the credits, then I was awarded a speech and debate scholarship to compete in public speaking and debate competitions.

I received an Associate of Arts Degree in Broadcasting on the same day that I graduated from High School and then in the summer, I started my third year of college and worked a few part-time jobs to have more money for my education.

Thanks to the fact that I had studied several languages, I was hired by Eastern Airlines in Miami as a Reservations Agent. The position was part-time at first but I was offered a full-time job if I would move to Chicago for the wintertime. I said there was no way I would possibly leave Florida for the winter but since I knew I had goals and needed to be self-sufficient and wanted insurance benefits, within 10 days I was living in Chicago and employed full-time.

Completing my college education was such a priority that I flew to college in Miami twice a week from Chicago. I was really the farthest commuting student attending Florida International University in Miami. I earned my Bachelor of Science Degree and then transferred back to Miami to work in the Springtime.

I mention all of this emphasis on education and how important it was to me because I want you to understand how hurtful it was to me when my boyfriend kept putting me down and telling me that education was not necessary.

8

FAST EXIT

After three years as an Airline Reservation Agent, I was promoted to the position of Airport Agent and worked in the Domestic and International Cargo Operations of Eastern Airlines at the Miami International Airport. Since most of the people in the department had seniority in the company and I was asked before being offered the position if I was willing to work any days and hours, I started on the graveyard shift with Monday and Tuesdays off.

I met a good looking, Latin Man from Venezuela in Miami at a Coconut Grove Nightclub. I was 21 at the time and working from 10pm-630am daily, getting home at around 7am. I loved music and dancing and since I didn't smoke, drink or do drugs, I had to have some release.

He was a great dancer, with a strong, sexy, hard, firm, muscular body. He was foreign, different and exciting. If only I didn't take him too seriously. Why do women want to get serious in a relationship?

He made time for his body and exercised every day. He kept up his incredible stamina by playing tennis every day and lifting weights. He exuded self-confidence and quite frankly, he was hotter than a jalepeño and he knew it.!

After about nine months together, I asked him if he was serious about our relationship and whether or not he loved me. He said he was serious and that he loved me and then he asked me to marry him. We went to the courthouse and got married. I loved a good adventure and was much more impulsive in those days.

During our second week of marital bliss, I decided to surprise my husband by taking a few hours off from work to get home and hop into our love nest around 3am, instead of 7 am.

Much to my surprise, our bed was a little crowded at that time with the blonde from the next door . Yes, she lived directly on the other side of the wall from our living room. I guess he didn't want to exert any effort to pick up someone from the next building over.

They were doing the regular neighborly thing while getting together during the hours I was working.

I was out the door before he could get his underwear on to run after me to explain. He could have said, "It's not what you think." I reserved a whole chapter for other men who have said just that and been caught lying later in the book.

You're right. It's not what I think that was distressing me, it's what I was seeing. Well if a picture paints 1,000 words, seeing my husband sharing intimate acts with the next-door neighbor said it all for me, thank-you. I left. Marriage over.

Luckily, the ink was barely dried on the Marriage License when the really good news (after the fact is always better to make a decision with) came that his divorce from his second wife in Venezuela had not been finalized prior to our marriage. He had two wives at the same time.

The judge did not find this humorous either and readily granted the annulment of the marriage. For the records, it never happened.

In case you're wondering about his track record......

His first wife in Venezuela was supposedly a wealthy woman and heir to a famous family fortune. He said she bought him a Mercedes Convertible as a wedding present. He was the one to ask for the divorce after she threatened to shoot him between the legs with a loaded gun when he came home from a long night of partying.

She suspected he might be cheating on her. He wasn't taking any chances of having his private parts blown off the map, so he had to go through with the action for divorce.

The girl in the apartment next door became wife number four. The neighborly activities in which they were engaged lead to the birth of their daughter. While he was married to her he applied for his green card so he could stay in the United States. When true marital bliss set in and his green card had arrived, they divorced.

At last report, he was single, still living in Miami. I wonder if he's still exercising every day? Moral of this chapter: If your mate is in great shape, make sure you know about his exercise routine!

9

HARD EXIT

Less than one year after the annulment, my best friend wanted to celebrate her birthday by going out dancing at a single's event at a Miami Beach Hotel. Can you just imagine where this chapter is going? I was not thrilled about going to this single's dance, but it was her birthday, her party so to speak. I had to go. I told her we wouldn't meet anyone at this particular resort.

Talk about eating your words. I just happened to meet the man I would marry that night. We hit it off so well. The sparks were flying and within four months I was saying, "I do."

For as long as I can remember, I loved public speaking and entertainment. I enjoyed creating and hosting events and had a definite flair for both of these things. My mother even insists that I was talking by ten months old. I must have had a lot to say, I still do, and had to get started talking early to get it all out.

Once we were married, my husband made it clear that he did not like the idea of me working unusual, late airline hours, since he was working mall retail hours. My seniority in the airlines had improved, but my hours were 2:30pm-11pm and that meant I wouldn't get home until about midnight. This was not a good idea for a newlywed couple in love, I remembered the last lesson, so I quit my job with the airlines after almost seven years and went into real estate.

I opted for self-employment in real estate and still kept creating , producing and hosting special events.

After giving birth to our son, I went back to selling real estate. The problems began when my son was getting sick in childcare. Our son was on antibiotics so often that my husband insisted that I take him out of childcare and stay home with him for six months to allow Craig's immune system to get stronger .

It was tough for me to stay home, I'd never done that before and my creativity was on a roll. Craig was an overly active child and demanded my constant attention.

I created events for nightclubs including fashion shows, parties, musical performances, beauty pageants and even bikini contests and earned $250 to $650 per hour. My husband liked that and said I should do it full-time.

He also never complained about having to see me work with models and there were no complaints about the bikini contests. Unfortunately, he wasn't a happy camper. He couldn't deal with stress and kept trying to think that my unique style should fit into his retail mall mentality. It is hard when someone believes that you work 40 hours a week somewhere, during certain hours and then come home with a certain amount of money and that's what should work the best.

He kept impressing upon me that I should take job, once Craig was getting bigger and healthier, that paid a definite amount of money. To appease him, I accepted a position as a Manager of a Real Estate Office, with a definite weekly salary and of course, you probably guessed already, I hated limiting my income to this amount. I knew in my heart that being on 100% commission was much better for me.

I already felt that life offered no guarantees, so if that was reality, why did I need a guarantee on my income? Why limit yourself? Make as much as you can. I liked the freedom of self-employment and being responsible for my own success.

Self-employment had less rules, more excitement and much more challenges.

The job of Real Estate Manager for someone else's firm was almost as emotionally abusive as the marriage. The corporate leader told me never to countermand his direct orders. In other words, I had to do whatever he wanted.....agree with his policies and practices, even when I disagreed.......this wouldn't work. I'd seen that picture before. I was doing my job well but I knew I wouldn't stay there.

I left the Manager's position to go back to being a commissioned salesperson. It was a good choice. To make a good living in real estate or any other commissioned sales position takes work and dedication of time plus building of clientele and referrals.

My husband had gotten to the point where he hated real estate. One day he told me to get a "real job." I remember so clearly telling him that I already had "a real job" and what I needed was "a real husband."

Things were going downhill between us faster than a snow skier on a slope. One night I was on the phone with a client discussing $1 million-dollar -plus homes and my husband just didn't want to hear even one more word about real estate. The client came over to visit and both of the men decided to go out for a few drinks.

When they walked out the door, a light went on inside of me, and the little voice said, "The exit's over there, use it." I reacted to my thoughts by opening the front door, then the car door, popping open the trunk and loading whatever fit that I thought my son and I would need. After taking the clothing and essentials, I got my son, put him in the carseat and drove off.

I left my husband a note that said, " I hope you'll be happier now." It must have been a mutually desired situation because he never contacted me about getting back together.

This was an extremely painful decision to make, but I didn't think I could honestly celebrate our upcoming 5th Wedding Anniversary . He didn't believe in me. This was devastating.

He was no longer supportive of the goals I wanted to achieve. He didn't want to accept me as a Creative Artist, with the need to express and use my creative talents. I concluded that to be anything less than myself was emotionally abusive. I was sure that time would not make our marriage better.

Since my husband and in-laws were no longer behind me, I decided it was best to put the marriage behind me, too.

10

A FEW THOUGHTS ..

If you think that there is a good possibility that you will be dead if you stay in a relationship, what would you have to lose by getting out? Is it that we prefer old habits to new challenges? Is fear the major issue? Is the fear of what we know a person will do less than the fear of the unknown?

Let's see... he'll just hit me once or twice and the.... Get real, he shouldn't touch you even once. Not ever!

Most of the time, leaving won't be easy. When a man knows that a woman wants to get out of a relationship he may try to do whatever it takes to prevent that from happening. Her challenges may range from the difficult to the seemingly impossible.

If he has money and can hold it back from her, he can make the exit more difficult. When my boyfriend knew that I was tired of his nonsense her made sure that he didn't purchase a piece of property he was interested in because the commission on this commercial transaction would have netted me more than $60,000 and he told me he knew that leaving him would not be a problem if I had that much money, so he didn't buy the property.

Jealousy, insecurity and anger are all issues to be dealt with. Some breakups are worse than others . Fatalities have occurred because of jealousy and we have had major news stories about spouses who couldn't cope with their partners leaving them.

How can a man make your exit difficult? No two exit situations are identical, but some of the elements may be similar. A man may attempt to make it hard for a woman by trying to cut off her communication with her friends and/or family members or anyone else he suspects might offer her help to leave him.

Money, as I mentioned, is a another issue of big concern for many women who are trying to get out of their situations. There are so many unhappy people in jobs today because they are scared to give up the income they receive from that job so that they can find something better.

Many men who are really weak human beings themselves get their strength by seeing their women weakened, dependent or helpless. Some men are physically violent, others are verbally abusive. Drugs and alcohol addictions or usage can intensify all of the problems.

Moving on to something new means that you experience a loss of what you are leaving behind. It is completely possible to be happy and depressed, all at the same time.

I think it's part of being a woman. You may have to mourn the past so that you can go ahead. We don't necessarily accept the fact that our relationships are over or should be.

Relationships: some men are too busy having a relationship with themselves, to have one with anyone else.

A girlfriend of mine was thrown out the back door of her home by her abusive husband. She told me she tried four times to leave him over a nine year period and she returned every time until the situation was absolutely unbearable.

After he flung her out the back door, she was finally ready to move away from him, get her own apartment and re-establish her life, without him. Then he must have realized that this time, she he You can imagine how shocked she was when he confronted her at one of the rental complexes. She had selected the apartment she wanted and was ready to sign the lease. He stole her purse. Her purse had the deposit she needed to move in.

Instead of doing whatever she had to do to continue with her plans to get away from him, she returned back home to her husband.

I was outraged when I heard about this episode. I couldn't understand what would make her go back to him. She was abused so badly over her nine year marriage that she did not have the confidence to just get away from him and believe that she would be just fine without him.

If fear of leaving is greater than the fear of staying, it is most probable that you will stay and suffer the consequences.Depending on how low your self-esteem has been dragged down from the abuse, you might even be convinced by your abuser, that you deserve to be mistreated and everything that is happening to you. It is not your fault , you don't deserve to be mistreated , ever or by anyone.

When you feel like you are the victim, you feel powerless. You are not powerless. You always have the power of your thoughts and the power to make decisions and choices. You have a responsibility to help yourself and your children, if you have any.

It will help if you can set priorities. Focus on what you want. Decide what is no longer acceptable, you can eliminate the negatives from your life. You can turn your upset and frustration into action. Once you are moving on this , things will happen. You can't stay stuck like SuperGlue and expects different results.

What do you want? Where do you want to be? Be determined that you will have the life you want .Make plans and prepare for the possible obstacles which may get in your way. Seek to be a role-model for your children, if you have any.

Change is such a big thing for most people. Did you know that doing nothing is really a decision? It requires a decision, a mental process, not to take any action. Let's make it clear that doing nothing will not change your life.

Decide to do something. Yes, through crisis as I mentioned before, we often are forced into a change. Action brings new things into you life and possibilities you have never thought existed.

It is so hard to understand why we just don't make changes until we absolutely have to, until we are literally forced into them. It's hard to understand why we wait so long.

11

BLOCKING THE EXIT

While going through my divorce, I stayed in the home of another woman who had also told her husband she wanted a divorce. He was a nasty, bad tempered worm. I can say that because it's the truth and besides, he lives in another country now and I won't divulge his name.

He wiggled his way back into the house and convinced her not to baby-sit for my son while I was working. Barbara had a two year old daughter, a perfect playmate and friend for my two year son.

Barbara was patient and a wonderful parent. It was Barbara who helped me potty train my son. I owe her many thanks.

Her husband asked me to move out within a few weeks of my arrival there. No correction, the creep told me to get out!

My presence in the house for emotional support and to share the bills with his wife were not a good thing for him. It was good for Barbara. I had to go because I was causing a disturbance in his plans of keeping her dependent on him, even if he was not a very nice person. My being in their house gave Barbara some money, which she desperately needed at the time so she could stay home and raise her daughter, while still keeping a roof over their heads. I also offered additional emotional support so she didn't feel so alone.

When her husband returned his goal was clear. At least I saw the situation very clearly. He wanted her dependent on him and he wanted to weaken her position. I provided strength. It is sad, but money can get in the way of clear thoughts.

In retrospect, I realize that I might have been in danger had I stayed because he had a bad temper. You never know what a person will do in a fit of rage.

Without enough money, it would not be easy to get rid of him. He was on the level of a cockroach. Too bad he wasn't a cockroach, we could have taken out the bug spray and eliminated the problem, but it wasn't that easy.

In case you were wondering, I ran into Barbara a few years ago during lunchtime at a restaurant. She informed me that she was a single mom and the Restaurant Manager, too. Her daughter was doing great and her ex-husband did everyone a favor by leaving the country. A happy ending. I love this sort of news.

I remember having another baby-sitter cancel on me because her husband refused to allow her to leave the house to make the money. He had a drinking problem which lead to fits of rage after a few drinks. He became dangerous and I knew she had to get away from him and his controlling influences and beatings.

The money she was planning on earning from the baby-sitting was to go back to school to improve her skills so she'd be more marketable when looking for a good paying job to support her two children. A job she would definitely need if she divorced him.

I knew she needed help. The not being able to get out of the house was a real clue. Hello, are you with me? Come in... hello.. As far as the physical abuse in the form of beatings, it is not acceptable to be beaten just because someone has had a few drinks. Physical abuse is totally unacceptable. There is no excuse for abuse.

I didn't know as much about abuse as I do today so I wasn't able to offer very much advice, but I called her as often as possible, especially if I thought he might not be home. I encouraged her to get help and recommended she exercise to reduce stress and make herself feel better.

At one point in my life, my stress level was so high, it took about three hours a day in the gym to calm down . Of course the results were a tight, firm, muscular body and renewed energy.

My baby-sitter didn't want to bring her marital problems out into the open. She continued to remain in denial.

I moved, we lost contact, but my prayers are with her and her children. Maybe one day she'll pick up this book, read this section and write to me to let me know she's on her own and doing fine.

12

CONTROL FREAKS

Some abusers could be considered "Control Freaks." To keep a woman they believe it is necessary to control everything about her life from the clothing she wears to the people she is permitted to associate with. They want to control the phone calls made and received, the places she can go and every detail about her life possible.

A controller can be so domineering in his desire to control the relationship that any deviation to his ideas and plans can set him on an emotionally charged course. Some men are phyiscally abusive others are verbal. Some are both.

In many of these cases, the controller will attempt to keep his partner surrounded by others who will not interfere with his controlling ways and not report him to the police or make waves.

Often a mother will keep quiet about her son's abusive, controlling relationship with his wife and make the excuse that her husband was the same way. Someone being controlled must get away from this circle of people and find people who can help or the abuse will continue.

A man who controls a woman in any of these ways might get extremely upset if she arrives home later than expected, gets a phone call from someone he doesn't know or she makes any statements that would indicate she has been thinking on her own.

A Controller preys on self-esteem. He may verbally batter you and tell you that you are no good; that there's nothing you will be able to do without him. He might ask, "What kind of job do you think you can get?" He might say, "You can't make it without me." He can make children the excuse for your having to stay home in statements like "I don't want the mother of our children working." He knows if you don't work you will be financially dependent on him and that's what he wants.

As long as you are dependent on him financially and you are weak emotionally, he has a chance of controlling your actions.

When he held me down in the bedroom he asked, "Are you going to do what I want?" The reply was always "Yes." He was a control freak.

In order for someone to abuse you, you must let him. Not leaving is permitting the abuse. Staying is the same as consenting to continued abuse. You can accept, reject or ignore anything written here, but the fact remains that to stay requires a decision to stay. Just like leaving requires a decision to go.

Once you stay after having experienced some form of abuse, repeating the abuse becomes easier for the abuser and worse for you.

Many women stay in abusive relationships because of fears. They are afraid that they don't have enough money, education, skills or confidence to change their lives. They stay. Time goes by. They experience more abuse. There are still there. One day something happens that makes them decide they can't or won't take any more abuse. Maybe it will be because they have read this book. It will take a strong reason to change their lives because they won't just change.

Many people are afraid of change. We cannot change anyone except ourselves. With this in mind, we might be better off getting away from a situation than trying to stay and change it.

When we move on, we may experience the loss of what we are leaving behind. It is possible to be happy and depressed at the same time. I know, I 've been there! We may have to mourn the past so that we can move on to the future. We don't always readily accept the fact that a relationship is or should be over.

If the fear of leaving is greater than the fear of staying, you will probably stay and take the consequences. Depending on how low your self-esteem has dropped, you might even be convinced that you deserve the abuse you are receiving and that in some way it is your fault. Rest assured, it is not your fault. It is his problem.

You have to power of your thoughts and the power of choice and must do everything in your power to use them and make choices.

13

SO THAT'S ABUSE

CLUES ON WHEN IT'S TIME TO GET OUT OF YOUR RELATIONSHIP

1. He's enjoying target practice and you're the target.

2. The only support you are getting is coming from your bra or pantyhose.

3. He won't let you sleep in the bedroom because he's afraid you'll use up his air.

4. He's holding a gun to your head while driving down the road at top speeds, threatening your life.

5. You can't balance your checkbook because he's locked it in the glove compartment of your car and taken the key.

6. He says he loves you so he bought you a present. He forgot to mention he charged the gift on your credit card or that you'll be receiving the bill soon!

7. You can't go anywhere because he didn't approve of the time you came home the last time you left, so he flattened all four of your tires.

8. He won't let you get a job because he's afraid that you'll leave him if you make any money.

9. When snap, crackled and popped describes your nerves . It's time to get out.

10. They garnish your wages to pay off his debts.

There is the possibility that you have not gotten away from an abusive situation or a relationship because it has not come to your attention that you are really being abused. What is abuse? Is there more than one type of abuse and can you experience more than one type of abuse at a time..?

Most people are more aware of physical abuse because it's signs can often be seen or heard. Physical abuse can include hitting, punching, slapping, grabbing, pushing, kicking, threatening violence and intimidating. Unwanted touching of a sexual or non-sexual nature is also physical abuse.

It is not unusual for a person to experience long-term mental or emotional abuse without others knowing. The signs don't have to be obvious that a person is suffering. It's sad, but true. In many cases, a relationship doesn't start out bad, it gets bad over time.

Emotional abuse occurs when there is a an attack on your self-esteem. Telling you that you are no good, useless, fat and ugly, incapable, stupid or worse is emotionally abusive. Verbal abuse with the intent of attacking your identity, autonomy, your sense of well-being, self-esteem, attempting to manipulate and control, isolate, force to do things against your will, putting you down continually. All of these are emotionally abusive.

Mental abuse and emotional abuse are very closely linked. When someone is trying to get to you and hurt you with their horrible words, it destroys your emotions and mentally hurts you. In it's severest form, you can't think clearly about what to do next or how to get away from the abuse. You fall apart mentally and emotionally from the burden of the emotional trauma of being abused. Drastic changes are necessary to get your life on a new track back to emotional health and towards happiness.

Hurting someone physically, mentally or emotionally does not solve any problems. It creates resentment and often hostility, not solutions.

I read this passage by a company known as Compassion Power and it is so true, " No one , under any circumstances, deserves to feel disregarded, insulted, controlled, coerced, intimidates, hurt , hit, pushed, grabbed or touched in any undesired way."

I found the Compassion Power site on the internet at : http://www.compassionpower.com and they offer all sorts of materials and classes about helping to heal from abuse.

14

IN ORDER TO EXIT, YOU HAVE TO ENTER

This incredible concept hit me like a ton of bricks: In order to make an exit, you first had to make an entrance.! This actually gives you power and control over your life if you believe it is true. If you don't get in to a situation.... you don't have to get out. It's your choice.

My mom used to tell me that we couldn't control everything in our lives but we could pick our friends and decide where to place our selves.

I met a man who was quite eccentric and an only child. He collected art and was a pro at self-promotion. He wrote his own press releases and had numerous articles about his collections in national publications. He had one major flaw.... He didn't like to share!

I don't know how he passed Kindergarten when he didn't master the art of sharing. It's such a basic requirement. "If I can afford to buy you your own can of soda, why would I share mine with you?" he wanted to know. He asked me out on a date. I felt his comment was a little strange, but I agreed to meet him anyway...

The little voice inside of me was already giving me an argument about this guy, but I proceed with my plans of getting together.

In addition to feeling a little concerned about how we would get along, I broke one of my own single-girl rules when he asked me to drive over to meet him at his place. I don't know why, but I agreed. He was so convincing, He was busy clipping out all these newspaper articles about himself that had appeared in 8 different newspapers that day......

He sounded so excited. Articles about his collections were appearing in all of those newspapers and he wanted to cut out the articles. Publicity like that would get me excited, so why should I listen to the little voice and think something was not right?

While driving on a major expressway to his place, it was raining so hard, I could hardly see the road. A really young driver in a vehicle in the far left lane lost control of his car and headed straight towards my car. In a fraction of a second, I saw this car coming right at me and to this day I'm not sure how I did it, but I got out of the vehicle so I wouldn't get killed. My car went into a ditch but I was alive to see it in the ditch , so I was thankful.

I quickly figured out that I had a totalled vehicle, that I was really far from home and that I needed to make a few calls. I called my date to see if he would pick me up and I was not prepared for his response: " Do you think you can find someone else to pick you up , I'm busy clipping out these articles from the newspaper and my flight leaves for Boston in the morning?"

The little voice inside of me screamed, " I told you so."

By the time the Fire and Rescue men arrived at the accident scene, I looked like a drenched rat in a sexy jumpsuit. The Rescue workers were really good looking and they offered to take me back to the station with them to wait for my father who agreed to get me, but the little voice inside of me was screaming by this point, " Haven't you had enough excitement for one evening?"

I could have sold one really great story about my date to the newspapers who had printed the good articles about him but instead I thanked God we weren't having a relationship. I didn't have a chance to make an entrance, so an exit wasn't necessary.

In case you were wondering: He called to see how I was doing... but the call came almost one year after the accident. It was nice he cared.(ha,ha).... Not sharing was the least of his problems. Just because a man has money, it doesn't mean he'll be nice to you.

15

SURPRISE EXIT

I have concluded that the reason I gave up my personal power and allowed myself to stay in a controlling relationship was money. A very wise woman told me that sometimes we don't know how much power we have until we give it up and then have to get it back.

Alone, with a two-year-old son to support, I knew I had my work cut out for me. My ex-husband agreed to give me $70 a week child support and for anyone out there who has tried supporting themselves and a child, you know that $70 a week does not provide a luxury lifestyle. That's why we call them "ex."

I was good at acquiring properties but in order for my boyfriend to cash out of his properties, someone would have to sell them. The woman who had those skills appeared about three years into our relationship to do just that plus take my business and boyfriend. I don't blame her for taking him, that was a mutual decision made by two consenting adults,

My big surprise came the day I came home from Graduate School after finishing my MBA. When my boyfriend greeted me in the driveway he said, "If you're leaving you might as well go now and you know, without me, you'll be eating out of garbage cans." He informed me that he rented out the house we were living in and that the new tenants had to move right in.

He did not take in to consideration where I would go with my son, just that he had received the money for the rental and that the tenants wanted it immediately. Bye. I had no time to think, it was a complete shock. He planned this and advertised the property. He knew how horrible he was going to be.

I suddenly had a flashback to the day I told him I had enrolled in the Executive MBA Program and he asked me upon hearing the news, Why do you need an education when you have money?"

I remember my response like it was yesterday, " You have money, because I have education. My education helped me to select all of your real estate investments and that's why you have money. My education is something that will stay with me when you leave." I've made plenty of mistakes, education was not one of them.

Apparently, I knew where this story was going to end, I just didn't know when and it took me more than four years to get the end of this relationship.

When the new tenants were moving in, I was extremely up-set. They were giving me a hard time about getting moved out so they could move in immediately. I was having a fit and was prob-ably on the verge of a nervous breakdown, but I never sought any medical professionals for my problems, I just tried to deal with them. Writing was my therapy.

Once again, I think that God provided the punchline because one of the new tenants, Bill, liked my legs more than my temper and eventually we started dating . God did not want me to be stranded, alone and hurting, so he sent me someone better. He sent me someone calm to deal with my storm. More about that later.

I found an apartment, packed and moved, but there was an unresolved matter between myself and my former boyfriend. I had given my boyfriend money towards the purchase of a prop-erty that he owned and he was refusing to give me my money back or to give me the deed.

With my business destroyed, actually to be taken over by this new woman, my roof over my head yanked out from underneath me, and the need to move on to something else, I needed the money back from this property or I needed to be given the title to the property so that I would know he couldn't take that away from me, too .

This was my life he was playing with, not a fast food restaurant where he could have everything his way, so I needed him to come to terms with me on this property issue.

Unfinished business needing to be resolved, I went to meet my former boyfriend at his new girlfriend's home, the place he was also moving, not that I was out of the way. At her home was a man I was told had come over to discuss investing more than $250,000 with my former boyfriend. While in her home I blurted out, " You don't want to do business with him, he's no good."

My honesty and candor outraged my ex-boyfriend. He freaked out at the thought of losing the $250,000 and in an adrenaline rush, he lifted me in the air and sent my 4'11" body flying through the front floor and then he threw me on the concrete driveway outside the house. What an exit!!

Bruised physically and emotionally, I was so enraged myself that he had taken physical actions against me that I went to the State Attorney's Office to file charges against him. This action ultimately helped me to get my money back from him, but not without having paid the emotional price.

At first, I feared retaliation from him and learned that the Florida laws were of no help in protecting many women who face physical abuse from someone. I wanted a Restraining Order to keep him away from me. The law stated that there had to be two incidents of problems with a person before you could get a restraining order. I knew that for some women, one confrontation could be deadly, who wanted to wait around and try it a few times. I was even more upset with the limitations of the laws. I absolutely felt in more danger than ever before.

To take other legal measures to obtain a Restraining Order meant spending around $2,000 in legal fees and that was not feasible at the time. It wouldn't have been a problem if he had given me back my $8,000 investment.

He finally gave me back my money and I dropped the charges and went on my way. The emotional pain lasted for much longer than I expected. I knew that one day I would write a book so powerful , that it would make more millions than I let slip away and that when I made this money, it was made because of my desire to share.

There is a desire to receive for one's self alone and he embodied that principal and then there is the desire to receive to be able to share. That's where I want to be so that can help others as well as myself.

The day this book hits the New York Times Best Sellers List, I am designing a 14k gold necklace with a diamond encrusted garbage can to wear as a reminder. I earned money but he didn't let me enjoy it. The best investment I made during our time together was in my education because it will last a lifetime. The best thing that he did for me was to force me out of his life . I just know that I deserved to fly First Class !

16

IT IS NOT WHAT YOU THINK

Some men are too busy having a relationship with
themselves, to have one with anyone else.

-Lori Wilk

One man told his wife that the credit card bill which arrived in
the mail reflecting a charge of more than $200 for a one-night stay
at a luxury resort was not what she thought. He claimed it was a
mistake. He admitted to being at the resort and said he was just
having a drink at the bar . The hotel made an error and charged
him this ridiculous amount for a hotel stay. He didn't stay there.
According to the husband, the charge was not correct and he was
going to call the resort and fix the problem immediately.

When the wife told me this story the hair stood up on my arms
and I got goosebumps all over my body. I looked at her and said,
"I don't know how to tell you this, but I'm getting a feeling that
he's cheating on you." A few weeks later she confirmed that my
feelings had been accurate. Her husband had cheated on her with
the Secretary from their business and they spent that night at the
resort. The charge on the card was his for the room.

What I think is that in addition to causing his wife emotional
pain he was stupid for not paying cash. Letting a bill for his inappropriate activities come to his house was even more abusive
than cheating.

For the wife, this information and documented credit card charge has given her the ability to make clear decisions based on verifiable facts and could be helpful in court if she needs to pursue a legal action against him.

17

SPEAKING OF ABUSE

If you decide to leave an abusive relationship, think of the Fire Safety Message:

GET OUT AND STAY OUT.
NEVER GO BACK IN.
YOU MIGHT NOT GET BACK OUT.

By now you know that I personally advocate getting out of undesirable situations as soon as possible.

I would not stay with anyone who abused me physically. All the therapy in the world would not give a man a second chance to hurt me.

Time is more valuable than anyone's money. Money can be replaced, time cannot.

Mental and emotional abuse often accompany physical abuse. Alone, their effects are less visible and often go undetected until the victim reaches the point of a nervous breakdown.(I'm talking about myself again!!!)

Figuring out how many people are suffering from emotional and/or mental abuse is almost impossible. The Mental Health Association estimates how many adults suffer from depression , but depression is only one symptom and just the tip of the iceberg.

If a woman goes to a medical facility for treatment of a physical abuse, the facility does not have to report the incident of abuse unless weapons were involved. Many black eyes and bruises have faded along with the fact that they ever happened and how.

Many people have pressures or are exposed to conditions which could trigger abusive scenarios including money problems, job issues or periods of unemployment, emotional stresses, alcohol or drug additions, gambling problems or losses, pregnancy,sexual problems, the lack of affection, loss of love, or even the loss or lack of self-esteem.

Any form of abuse can reduce a woman's self-esteem and confidence levels and make it harder for her to get them back. Abuse can cause anger, frustration, stress, fear, panic, desperation , pain or lead to other addictions or abuses as forms of escape including alcohol, cigarettes, drugs or even eating disorders. Not to mention a headache or two.

Let me share a few more situations which were mentally, physically or emotionally abusive.

WE'VE TAKEN ENOUGH

I beg you to leave
but you say it's no use
so you hang around
and take his abuse.

You know it's a fact
that he's hitting you
but when prosecutors ask
you say it's not true.

That's the problem
we are faced with today
we suffer abuse
the men get away .

We've taken enough
enough of their "wit"
men have to know
they can't bite or hit.

Put them in jail
throw away the key
make life safer
for our families.

We have the power
to make this come true
taking the first step
is still up to you.

Let's get together
let's work as one
and stick together
to get the job done!

-LORI WILK

18

TWO FROM COLUMN A

PAIN PLUS A FEW YEARS EQUALS COMEDY

When you can finally laugh at the things which caused you pain, you have a pretty good sign that you are healing emotionally.

I'm probably like many girls, my parents gave me the impression while I was growing up that I should one day marry a successful man. The successful men were doctors, lawyers and business chiefs. I took this advice and tried dating some doctors, lawyers and corporate leaders. It proved to be an adventure, not an avenue.

I got away from my abusive situation and decided to go out with a nice Doctor... every mom's dream for her daughter, right???

We were at his home when the doorbell rang. When he answered, I heard a Chinese woman's voice, "Oh honey, how nice, you ordered us Chinese food," I replied.

I got the Chinese part right, but she didn't bring any food with her.

This was my clue that she wanted to see the doctor, too and since visiting hours were over and this was his home, not the office, I quickly put two and two together and came up with good-bye!

We talked about sharing before... the soda, the pizza, but not a man. Of course since his ego was enjoying this more than my temper, I decided that if he wanted Chinese, who was I to stand in his way.

When it comes to a man, one good one is enough. Now if only I could find one good one!

Fast Forward Five Years .....

The doctor is now engaged to get married. Not to the Chinese girl, either. He's decided to stick to one dish. Besides, the best way to attract a doctor nowadays is not to be sick and not to tell him you're single. Tell him you have good medical coverage and you're in. And probably for more than one appointment.

19

CALCULATED EXIT

"I figured it was time to leave."

-Lori Wilk

This book is about getting out of situations which are mentally, physically or emotionally abusive and until now, I've been writing about relationships and I'd like to acknowledge that these problems are not limited to relationships. It is possible and I am sure that many people work in environments and with people who are abusive. Let's talk about some of those scenarios.

Today everything is so instant, that many time, people end their situations in an instant manner. I have had people tell me that they were notified of a break up in their relationships via e-mail or fax. The breakups were fast, but cold and hard to cope with emotionally. Many of these instant endings caused severe emotional trauma for the person on the receiving end of the e-mails or faxes.

It's time to talk about work related issues. When it comes to working in abusive environments, sometimes the best thing you can do is find something else to do!

As a motivational speaker, I always begin my presentations with the disclaimer that when I speak, I don't hold anything back. I don't tone down the message to make it easier to accept. Some people have gotten so motivated by my messages that they have taken action and quit their jobs and I don't apologize.

When I worked for the airlines, I had a Manager who told me that if I didn't shut up, he would pick me up and throw me through the window I was standing next to and I had the nerve to respond to him with.."If you're going to do it, you might as well do it now." Of course, I had a whole group of witnesses standing there and he didn't throw me through the window, but I can say I was helpful in helping him find a new career path because he left the company, I mean he was fired, shortly after.

Not everyone will like what you say, but sometimes you have to say it anyway.

I have not chosen to flow smoothly over the flowing brook, I have decided to take the rapids. As I get older, I am walking more in the streams and trying to get away from the volcanoes. I am seeking a different more calm path, but don't think I 'll shut up any time soon. God willing.

A few years ago I was experiencing car difficulties, so I drove into a local car dealership to their service center. It was a stressful mess which kept me there for about 40 hours over a five day period and got me so angry that I confronted the General Manager of the dealership to help me with my concerns.

This General Manager was impressed with my persistence and he told me I should be selling cars. I told him that I didn't know the first thing about cars, but he didn't know that I wanted to know what the car selling game was all about because as far as I was concerned, as soon as I learned the game, that would be the last time any one of those car dealers would have the advantage in a transaction with me.

The General Manager said they would teach me about the cars and asked if I wanted a position selling cars at his dealership. I accepted the challenge. Not only did I think it could be fun. I was not intimidated by the men and I knew they would be surprised because I would make money selling cars. Probably more than they were expecting. This was another educational opportunity with benefits I could use for a lifetime. I started training for the position as a New Car Salesperson almost immediately.

In the course of my employment as a New Car Salesperson, I met many people who were interested in purchasing a car and quite a few of these potential buyers had questions they wanted answered before entering into the agreement to make this major purchase.

More than 90 percent of the new cars I was selling were priced at more than $10,000 and at least 50 percent of them were more than $15,000. I am sure that I sold many cars that cost more than some of the people earned for the entire year and yet the dealership expected the customers to decide instantly to commit to these high dollar, long term payment purchases.

This was a big decision I was helping people with. My attitude was that I was there to make money while helping these people. I didn't want them to regret their purchase the next day or the next week when the payment book arrived.

I even expected to received referrals from satisfied customers who were happy with my service. I knew that referrals would help my income grow and that having a good reputation was important. I wanted to help people make good informed decisions and yes, that included buying or leasing a vehicle.

From years of experience in the real estate industry, I knew that the major purchases that people make in their lives are their home and their transportation. If handled wisely, they could be great. If mistakes were made, they'd be stuck for a long time with the mistakes. Homes and cars are not chewing gum or coffee. I wanted to help people make good decisions. One's they could live with a long time.

How I handled myself was unacceptable to my employer. In real estate I got comfortable working with my Hewlett Packard HP 12c financial calculator to figure out loan payments and interest rates and other financial things. I carried my financial calculator in the pocket of my business suit to work. It was a very helpful tool when customers had financial questions and concerns before entering into a contract to purchase a vehicle. Can you imagine where this is going???

The car dealership did not share my customer service philosophy which included providing information to potential buyers before they arrived at the finance department. According to my bosses, financial information was not anything I should discuss with my customers before they signed the purchase agreement.

I was not the Finance Dept., I couldn't quote interest rates or run credit reports, but I was well qualified with my MBA, maybe even more qualified than some of the men in the Finance Dept. at explaining the difference between paying on something for six years and being upside down or building up equity.

My focus was a long-term customer with referrals, theirs was instant gratification and the rest wasn't a priority. At first, I was told to put the calculator away. I did not use the HP 12c all the time, only when I felt that by giving the customer an idea of what to expect in terms of money, when I felt it would help me make the sale, then I turned to my trusty calculator.

I also used my financial knowledge to help the dealership structure a sale in a manner they had never tried before so that they could make the sale. They took my advice and then they felt they were waiting too long for the customer to get her permanent car loan so they told me not to come back to work until I had repossessed the vehicle I sold her. At 4'11" I don't think I'm taking anyone's car and besides, that definitely wasn't the job of a new car salesperson. I was also given the ultimatum by my bosses: Leave the calculator at home or leave the company. My calculator and I figured it was time to go....

In case you were wondering:

The car dealership repossessed the vehicle. The customer finally received her financing and returned to the dealership to buy, not one, but two cars from me. I was no longer a New Car Salesperson. To that I say.... where's my commission?

I considered working at another car dealership a few years ago when I wanted to generate some fast, good income and the hiring manager said that they don't like to hire woman because they are not usually successful in the car business. Women just don't have what it takes to go after the business like the guys do. The only women they hire as he continued to explain to me were those that kept calling back to beg him for the position and try to convince him that they really wanted the job.

Needless to say, I didn't want to work for this company and I wasn't in a fighting mood to lodge complaints with the Equal Employment Opportunity Commission about this company, but it scares me to know that there will be people who beg for these jobs and end up enduring emotional if not verbal abuse from him. Abuse continues in the workplace and we're almost at the year 2000.

In this case, avoiding further exposure to abuse was the best thing I could do.

20

YOU HAVE TO....

If you're like most people, you probably can't stand having someone tell you that you "have to" do anything. We know that we "have to" die eventually and the IRS says we "have to" pay if we have a certain amount of taxable income. Aside from those, there are not too many other things we absolutely "have to" do.

Have you ever heard anyone say: "you have to" because "I said so?" In the adult world, doing something just because someone "says so" might not be a good enough reason to comply. Life is about choices ; some of which will effect us in a major way and some which won't..

Blindly obeying commands " you have to" or because " I said so" can land you in jail even if they come from your employer, if you are told to do something unethical or illegal and y ou follow the orders.

It helps to be able to think clearly when making major decisions . You might not be thinking clearly if you are under severe stress.

You should not be forced to do something illegal or which compromises your integrity.. You should not be threatened or given ultimatums to do something or else you will be fired. If you are being threatened, you are being abused. Get help get away from the abuse.

There have been cases of women being told they have to comply with sexual requests from their employer or be subject to losing their jobs. This is not only abusive it's also sexual harassment.

My ex-husband preferred the security of a paycheck to the risk of running his own business. My father, the business-man, taught me that to get anywhere in life required risks and perseverance. No risk, no reward. I learned to associate more danger with driving to work than in changing jobs, careers , relationships or situations.

I had an employer who said that "I had to" do certain things. He had a valid point and he was correct , in his own way. If I wanted to continue working for his organization and to keep re-ceiving paychecks there, I had to follow his direct orders.

The good news: I had the "right to" decide if I wanted to continue working for him. I didn't "have to". Money is great and it helps with many things, but it's not the only "reason to" do things.

As you might have already guessed, I did not choose to con-tinue working for a company which did not allow me the freedom of using my brain to make decisions.

If someone is holding a gun to your head, you might have to cooperate temporarily. If he is holding you down and asks if you are going to do what he wants, you might at that moment agree with him under the circumstances and say " yes."

You have the controlling power over yourself and your deci-sions and the responsibility to decide what to do to proceed with your life. Don't give away your power and let someone hurt you by making you believe that you have no choice or that you " have to" do anything.

21

EXIT NOW, AVOID THE RUSH

Sooner or later, your light will turn green, even if right this moment you still see red. My question is, Why not exit now and avoid the rush? Go with a clear head, not a black eye. It is easier to leave when things are calm and not chaotic. Go, before you are forced out.

Do you think that termites would rather fly out of the wood in a house freely or fight and struggle to their death once the fumigation tent has been placed over the house and the gas is being pumped in?

Things are always more hectic the last minute when you have to rush to get away. You may have heard stories about people in South Florida who stayed inside their homes during Hurricane Andrew almost 6 years ago.

Many people thought their homes were safe and that they didn't have to worry about the forces of a hurricane hitting them. Their home would always be the safest place to be. In reality, the winds exceeded the 115 mile per hour mark in many places and the results of staying in their homes were often devastating, life threatening and down right scary for many people who just couldn't bring themselves to consider the reality that sometimes you have to go away from what you know or are used to.

Sometimes you have to exit and leave material things behind in order to protect yourself and your loved ones.

People are more important than property. Money can replace possessions, but the old saying is still true, "You can't buy happiness." Yes, some people rent it temporarily. Many of us if not most of us, allow money to influence our decisions for many reasons.

22

MYTHS

Some Thoughts About Garbage:

1. Once garbage is removed from your home, it usually doesn't come back.

2. Garbage is not usually something you want to save.

3. Garbage is taking up space which could be used for something else.

4. Your trash might be someone else's treasure. Let them have it.

Myth #1

If you ignore the problem, it will go away.

Ignoring a rip in your pantyhose will not make it go away. As the day goes on, the rip tends to get bigger, more noticeable. We don't always want to look at our situations too carefully because we don't want to notice the rips and tears or to admit that we have a real problem that just won't go away.

Myth #2

Things have to get better.

Who says? It often takes a crisis for people to make changes in their lives. Through crisis comes change because anything less than a crisis does not necessarily jolt anyone into action. The key word here is action. We wait until the fire is burning up the house to get out. We often wait until we are fired before we look for a new job.

Myth #3

I can leave at any time. It's not an emergency. Now is not a good time.

Reality check: If your situation becomes an emergency, you might be leaving, but not in your own car... It might be an ambulance. Domestic violence is a reality. Every 7.4 seconds a woman is abused. How long did you say you are going to wait?

Myth #4

I am the one who is doing something wrong. All of this is my fault.

It's time to get off the guilt trip and out the door. Guilt is a trap. Fear is a crutch. Low self-esteem, combined with insecurity and fear can be holding you from walking out the door. Walk out the door anyway.

Myth #5

I have to stay because of the children.
This is one of the worst excuses. Sorry. Most children have eyes, ears and feelings and they will see, hear and feel your pain.

By staying, you make your children victims of abuse both mental and emotional . A very high percentage of children are abused in the households where one of their parents is abused.

A woman once told me that " If mama's not happy, nobody's happy." You've got to please yourself first before you can help your children.

Children don't just view abuse and forget. The images of the abuse and emotional scars will be there for many years , if not a lifetime. Children may grow up with guilt, physical or emotional scars, frustrations and confusion because they were exposed to abuse.

Abuse can't hide behind walls or doors. Children often can and do hear their parents fighting and arguing. Too often, they see the abuse. They feel helpless. Depending on the age of the children , they may even feel personally responsible for their parent's problems.

As the adult, you are responsible for changing the situation. As a parent, you should love and protect your child from abusive situations. By staying, you may be making your children victims of abuse. Leave for yourself and for your children.

23

NO TOLL THIS EXIT

On some roads you have a chance to exit before you have to pay the toll. On the road of life, I believe we pay all the way. There's no free exit, no free space like on a Bingo card.

Every exit makes you pay with change. Change brings new things and it also brings a sense of loss or even mourning for the loss of some of the old things you might be leaving behind.

The nation watched the O.J. Simpson Trial. He was abusive at various times during his marriage but we also saw pictures of happy times. Bad situations are not 100% bad and not 100% abusive. Sometimes this is hard to comprehend.

In any bad situation, there can still be a sense of loss over the positive aspects of the relationship. We can feel sad, confused , scared and happy, all at the same time.

There can be emotional pain when making changes because we are giving up something familiar or leaving something behind to make the change. In families, if moves are involved, losses can include not being able to take the family pet to the new place of residence. This is traumatic for the children and parents. Some things you will leave behind are bad but they are at least familiar bad things.

Some of the anxiety in the change comes from the fear of the unknown. Yes, it is not unusual to be afraid when you don't know what will happen next. When you drive down a highway for the first time, it seems strange and you might be worried if you are even headed in the right direction. It often takes longer to get somewhere for the first time than it will ever take to get there again. The drive home always seems much faster once you've been there.

24

CONSIDERATIONS BEFORE EXITING

There can be many things and issues you consider before you get out of a relationship or situation that is no longer serving your highest purpose. They include but are not limited to "fears, finances and feelings. " Let's consider them, one at a time.

We'll start with our fears. First we can have fears for our physical safety. Physical safety for yourself and your children, if you have children is extremely important and definitely one of the first concerns you might face. Fears, if out of control, can become major roadblocks and can keep you from starting on the path to the life you want. Some people say they almost feel immobilized by their fears, stuck like Super Glue, unable to move ahead , get out or go anywhere.

Please, ask yourself, "Do I believe that I will be in danger when and if I leave this household and person?" If you have reason to believe that your life will be in jeopardy, be all means, seek additional security and take precautions to protect yourself and your family. Document anything that makes you feel insecure and tell a friend, family members, the police, a lawyer , an abuse hotline or anyone you deem necessary about these safety concerns.

According to the American Bar Association, it is not uncommon for a woman to be in more danger after leaving an abuser than when with him because the abuser often can become more outraged at the thought of losing control of the situation than when you are with him.

Pay attention and make a written documented trail about any weapons that you know your partner may have in his possession which could be used or potentially used in a bad situation. If your physical well-being is in danger, it may be necessary to consider obtaining legal protection in the form of Restraining Orders or physical protection with a bodyguard.

I have met women who were married or in relationships with high-powered or wealthy men. Many found it necessary to take measures to hide or to be protected while they were working out their problems and trying to re-establish their lives.

It can be a mistake to underestimate the lengths an enraged man may go to cause a woman trouble or to physically harm her, if he can find her.

You never know what another person is going to do so it may help to consider the nature of the person you are with and to take whatever precautions you can

If you need suggestions or need to talk to someone about some of the possibilities and this is overwhelming to you, please know that you are not alone. One of the toll-free numbers you can call is the National Domestic Abuse Hotline at 1-800-799-Safe.

You might consider a Safe House, a Shelter , a hotel stay or even staying with friends or family, but please get help.

It is important to consider where you will stay if you want to get away and if you do consider some type of shelter or residence, you may want to consider one outside your current city, county or state. Sometimes, distance makes getting to you or finding you or causing you more grief harder and more complicated for the person you are trying to get away from.

Ask yourself, "What is the mental and emotional state of the person I want to leave?" Is he addicted to drugs, alcohol, have a history of depression or a criminal record."

If you are employed, does your employer have any emergency programs you can contact that can help advise you so that you can continue to work while you take care of your problems? Is there a counseling program you can contact and is it free of charge or is it fee based?

Considerations Before Exiting

Have you contacted your local United Way to ask about any local organizations or support groups they know about or support which might be helpful for you?

I have included a Resource Guide at the back of the book which has more information and phone numbers and even websites which can be reasearched for possible helpful leads, hints or tips. The Resource Guide is only the tip of the iceberg of information about this topic. A complete guide could many books. Also, resources do change, so they are only meant as a positive additional and this book or author makes no guarantees about what any service or organization might or might no do to help you with your personal situation.

When it comes to survival, starting with the basics: a roof over our head, we need money. It might help to make a list of what you will need to start over so that you can create a budget and review your finances to determine what you have to work with to get you through a transition period.

You will want to consider the cost of temporary housing, permanent housing -deposits for rental or purchase, deposits for utilities, a few months rent or closing costs for a purchase, food expense, transportation, clothing, legal, accounting, utilities, school expenses, medical expenses and even clothing and sundries.

Ask yourself if you have any family or friends who can help you. Are you working and can you continue in this position or will you need to change employers or make other income arrangement? Will you need child care facilities for your children so that you can work extra hours to cover some of your expenses or babysitters to give you time to take care of some of the details of this transition?

Do you have to sell any assets to be able to afford to change your life? Do you have to get rid of any high payments, like a house payment, a car payment, credit card debts or other expenses? How will you secure the cash you need for this situation if a move is necessary?

Do you have any other assets which you can convert to cash or borrow against? Do you have any untapped lines of credit, stocks, bonds, savings, an insurance policy or an employee Credit Union which makes loans?

Have you consulted a lawyer or an accountant ? Money is a personal thing, but a little planning can save you from experiencing even more stress at an already difficult time.

You've considered some safety and financial issues, what about some of the emotional issues surrounding your feelings.

In emotional times, we don't think as clearly as when we are not as stressed or under so much pressure. Do you have the emotional support and mental preparedness to make changes in your situation? Is was not aware that I was on the verge of a nervous breakdown at the end of an abusive four year relationship. I was a devastated mess . I yelled , screamed and cried frequently. I wish there was someone who had written a book like this when I needed it.

To get the emotional support you need , have you considered joining a support group or do you have family or friends who can help you. I have to stress here having people who can help you, not criticize you or put you down-support you and help build you up again. There are many resources available and if you have questions, even a call to you local Mental Health Association can be positive for information, referrals and assistance.

Are you depressed? Are you aware of the tendencies of abuse victims to also be abusive of their children? If you are in stress, it is also most likely that your children are experiencing some stress of their own and any positive addition to their lives will be helpful. It is hard to be careful not to add more pressure to the children than they are experiencing.

Make sure you can take care of yourself and your emotions so you in turn can take care of your children, if you have any. One way to release some pressure in your life is to find some time to think. A good way to do this is to take walks, for whatever length of time you can manage-20 minutes or more is very theraputic. As you walk, your body not only feels better, you get a chance to think. Take your child for a walk with you if you can and you can be together , get calmer and clearer about what you are doing and it is great for both of you.

It is important to feel good about yourself. A decision to have the life you desire and improve your life is a big step. Appreciate yourself and pamper yourself in any way you can find possible. It doesn't have to be complicated. Honor yourself with a relaxing bath or polish your nails. Do something to make yourself feel good.

Turn on the radio and dance to music that you enjoy. Do something that makes you feel good and happy.

The next consideration I call facing reality . This is about realizing that you have a problem and dealing with it, by planning and seeking help for the questions and problems you can't handle alone. When you plan out how you will handle your situation , you will feel more confident and less afraid. Planning will give you a sense of direction instead of distress.

There are many organizations which offer help for your various problems, there are websites where you can research more information as well as find chat groups for support. There are numbers to call for help, so please ask for help if you need it.

I am not a doctor, so I don't offer any medical advice . I can only suggest that anyone who needs help seek professional assistance for their mental or physical concerns.

25

MORE THOUGHTS

In most cases, the abuse just won't stop without some type of help in resolving the underlying problems. In many cases, if the police are called to respond to a domestic violence complaint, they will not get the results they had hoped for. They often leave the scene only to have to wait to be called again, often to return to a more serious incident.

A 1992 Time Magazine article, "When Violence Hits Home," gave the statistic that according to an American Medical Association report, as many as 1 in 3 women will be assaulted by a domestic partner in her lifetime. This represents approximately 4 million woman in any given year who will be assaulted.

We can be honest and admit that money is one of the biggest factors in divorce and also abuse. Money is an issue for most adults whether they have very little or quite a lot. People want money, they don't like losing it and will often do crazy things to get it or to keep from losing it. When a man is forced to pay child support and/or alimony it can make him behave differently towards the woman who initiated this action against him.

As human beings, we also want someone to love us. We take to heart what our loved ones say to us and how they respond to us and our needs, whether they are telling us we are beautiful or something mean. Personal attacks on our self-esteem can be emotionally debilitating for men and women.

If a man believes that he is going to lose a woman he wants, he may become abusive in an attempt to regain some level of control over her. Some men don't know how to handle rejection. We have heard statements like, "If I can't have her, nobody will."

We can accept, reject or ignore the realities of our own lives. Ultimately, we must decide for ourselves where to stay in our situations or relationships or move on.

Everywhere I go, I talk to women about their lives and their relationships. I have met so many incredible women while writing this book. So many woman have told me that their husbands or boyfriends have told them they couldn't make it without them and survive on their own.

The truth is that so many women have made it and can make it and are on the road to a much better life without their abusive relationships draining their emotions and taking their lives away. I meet woman who will do whatever it takes to be successful, so themselves and their children and I applaud them for taking the steps to make it happen.

We woman often go through quite a lot with our men, here's a few examples. One of my Realtor friends sold a house in Ft. Lauderdale, on the intracoastal and the owner of the house included a boat in the sale. The boat was included in the sale of the home because the boat had been delivered back to the dock by the Coast Guard after the husband died on board while having an affair. The mistress arrived at the dock with the boat but the wife didn't want to have any part of this boat, so she gave it to the new owners- a nice $50,000 present.

In Georgia, a businessman was interested in an Exotic Dancer he saw perform at a local club. He was so entranced by this dancer that he walked out on his wife of 25 years and bought a home with the dancer and fathered a child with her. Within a few months of the birth of the child, he suffered a massive heart attack and the dancer no longer wanted him. He begged his ex-wife to take him back so that he wouldn't lose his business.

A Dental Hygienist was working in New York and rearranged her cleaning around the snow storms to get home before the storm hit. When she arrived early she found her husband in bed with the babysitter.

It's amazing what happens in our relationships.

26

WHAT WERE THEY THINKING ?

Just before I published this book, two articles appeared in the Thursday April 29, 1999 edition of the Orlando Sentinel, they were about cases of severe physical, emotional and mental abuse. These dramatic, horrible stories are about incidents which happened to real women in Florida.

I mentioned earlier in the book that men often go emotionally bonkers when they come to the end of a relationship. Some get so angry at losing control and losing their women and often their children that there is no telling what they will do. Some men get very dangerous and I can't emphasize enough that caution may be necessary in dealing with them during and after a break up.

I cried when I read about these women and my prayers go out to them. The first article is about a woman whose ex- husband went to jail 18 years ago for attempting to murder her. This story was in the news because she recently asked the Parole Commission to never release her ex-husband from prison. His parole date is not until the year 2017, but she considers him so dangerous, she is fighting to keep him behind bars. She decided that now is the time to start to make sure he won't get out.

Even though he has been behind bars for the last 18 years , he has been sending her death threats in the mail. He has also threatened the judge and the prosecutor in this case. He has been warned not to write and send any more threatening letters.

He is serving a 114-year sentence for attempted murder of his ex- wife. He attempted to kill her directly in front of the Hillsborough County Courthouse 18 years ago when she arrived there to testify against him in a probation violation case. She also planned on testifying that he abused their baby by burning him with cigarettes and biting him. He was enraged that she showed up at the Courthouse ready to testify, so he poured a container full of gasoline on her and set her on fire.

She was horribly burned and disfigured and has endured numerous surgeries to help correct the damage done to her appearance. She has suffered extensively.

The second article is about a woman who may be in immediate danger if a judge releases her estranged husband from jail any time soon. This man is currently behind bars charged with attempted first-degree murder, kidnapping, aggravated battery and aggravated assault.

When his wife came to pick up their daughter, he grabbed her and did mean things before the police could arrive and when the police arrived he decided that it was time to kill her, so he shot her in the chest. When he realized she wasn't dead, he shot her in the hip and poured hydrochloric acid over her head. The acid got into her eyes and burned her whole upper body.

According the article, the man told his wife he planned on killing her for ruining his life and he said that he couldn't cope with paying her child support for their daughter or with the idea that she might be with someone else.

A controller who loses control can be devastated. The results are often deadly as I have stated before in this book and backed up with statistics.

This man has asked to be released from jail on bond. This woman fears for her life. This man's attorney is trying to make the case that his client is mentally ill and should be released from jail for treatment.

It is my opinion that the name of the judges who make these decisions should be released to the public along with their decision so that we can make better decisions when we go to the polls and vote.

My verdict is to keep him behind bars. Let's see what the judge decides. Follow-up in my next book about abuse. I cannot forget my own desire to obtain a Restraining Order and learning that I had to experience two incidents of abuse before I could apply without separately hiring an Attorney to go through more red tape. Once is more than enough.

27

HE ENTERED THROUGH MY EXIT

Some things are funny. Some things are probably not a coincidence. Some things are probably meant to be. I have learned that pain plus time equals comedy. You need time because at first, these horrible things don't seem very funny.

You might remember my comments about one of the new tenants, Bill, who rented the house I was thrown out of. Well I said that he seemed more interested in my legs than in my temper.

Bill entered through my exit. Bill respects and appreciates my talents and would not stand in the way of my happiness or success. We got along very well once we met for a second time under different circumstances and we have been together ever since, almost eight years.

My ex-boyfriend gets all the credit for this move. Like ordering a pizza, exactly the way you want it and having it delivered to your door. He delivered Bill to my front door and even screened him for acceptability. This was his idea of ruining my life.

My ex-boyfriend thought he was making all the decisions in this breakup but I would like to think that maybe there was some heavenly intervention in selecting the cast and directing the show.

28

JUST WHEN YOU THOUGHT
IT WAS OVER

When I thought I had finished writing this book, I realized that there was so much more to say. Men and women read the manuscript for this book and came up with questions they felt needed answering, more ideas that could be explored.

As a woman, I presented this story from a woman's point of view, but was willing to listen to the various male responses to my writing and I wanted to respond to some of their questions.

Not surprising was the statement of many men that they could see themselves in this story and they too had done some of the things which I thought were wrong.

I watched a recent episode of the television show "20/20" in which the lead story was about the disappearance of a girl named Amy, more than 18 years ago. I knew her brother. She has never been found. No one really knows what happened to her but there have been reports that she was horribly abused and other reports that she was even killed after being tortured.

What is known is that a man made obscene, abusive phone calls to Amy's mother for all these years and subjected the mother to intense, unimaginable emotional and mental pain. Pain that was in addition to the pain she was experiencing from searching and not knowing what happened to her daughter.

Maybe by bringing this story to the attention of the public on such a widely viewed national show information will surface which will help find Amy. My prayers go out to her and her family.

Also on this show, was a story about a Baptist Minister who started a program in the Churches about five years ago called "Sister, I'm Sorry." In this program, men, say they are sorry to women who have been abused, not specifically by them , but abused none the less. The women receive apologies from men which helps them on the road to emotional recovery and healing. Men release the pain and heal by apologizing. There is so much work to do to stop abuse, there will never be too many people doing it.

Men have asked me why I advocate women leaving their men without suggesting they seek counseling or help to work out their problems first. This was insightful but I say that leaving is my personal choice, each person has to decide what is right for them. If a man is treating me incorrectly, he has to want to stop the behavior. The wanting to stop comes before even getting help to stop.

When it comes to the issue of physical abuse, I don't believe it should be permitted even once and once permitted, I think it becomes easier for the abuser to hit you again and take more severe actions. I believe that violence doesn't get any prettier and is most likely to escalate. I am not about to wait and test the waters . The more acts of violence a woman is subjected to, the more likely she will become seriously injured or killed. I would recommend getting out of the path of physical abuse as quickly as possible.

I have read articles that indicated that most men won't voluntarily go to batterer's programs, they have to be forced to go. There are too many men, possibly due to their upbringing or cultural backgrounds who have experienced abuse in their households while growing up. Some of these men do not think that there is a problem with hitting their wives, their girlfriends or even their children.

Unfortunately, too many men don't think that hitting is abusive. Some men even state that they think the women deserve to be hit. Confronting a man about his abusiveness can be dangerous.

To get a man's attention can an often does take a court order or being thrown in jail. One mother of six was interviewed on a Central Florida radio station in December. She has gotten away from an abusive husband and asked the radio station to grant her wish of having a Christmas Tree and gifts for her six children.

The radio station provided the tree and presents and she told the listening audience that her husband had held her at gunpoint in his car, pulled the trigger and then pushed her out the door at more than 55mph. He was behind bars for attempted murder. She is alive but alone now with six children to support.

I have included a Resource Guide at the back of this book which lists phone numbers throughout the country of Abuse Hotlines in case any of my readers want to speak to someone about their problems or to give these numbers to a friend or family member who needs them.

Men helped me to understand some of their challenges and circumstances which could lead up to some of their abusive behaviors. Men indicated that life changes drastically when they get married. If they have a high sex drive while dating, it doesn't just drop because they get married. They still want sex and some men still want it as often as they were getting it while they were single. Tensions often arise. Woman might want more, too.

Now add children to the equation plus money and job pressures and a man might have a wife who is worried about the children and the money and the realities of running a household and she might not be extremely interested in making love. She might be more ready for an Extra Strength headache remedy than sex at the end of the day. This applies to both men and women. He might be ready for a beer or something stronger. Pressures mount and people who can't cope often find escapes in drugs, alcohol and cigarettes. The escape items don't solve the problem, they just push them below the surface so as not to be seen clearly or dealt with.

So how does a man respond to his desire for more sex? In some cases, he takes it, like a cave man and is accused of marital rape. Date rape is also a big problem for college students and teens. Sometimes, his hormone levels build up and he drinks excessively or abuses drugs and he gets angry or frustrated until the point at which he emotionally snaps.

When he snaps, he may hit , injure or kill his wife and also hurt his children . So many people can't cope with the pressures of their lives. They need help but never ask for it and never receive it.

Upbringing and experiences effect attitudes. A man who has been brought up in a household where his mother was abused might not really know what is right or how to handle his own relationships.

Statistics show that half of all rapes of women over 30 are part of the battering syndrome. For women as a whole, battering is a factor in 35 percent of all rapes.

When a woman leaves a man, he sometimes gets angrier, more upset and violent. In almost 3/4 of the reported spouse assaults, the victims were separated or divorced from their abuser at the time of the incident. Battered women are often at greater risk when they leave their abuser.

I think there should be a law requiring any abuser to get treatment in a specialized program once a legal separation or divorce proceeding has taken place. This would help circumvent their taking matters in their own hands and acting on their rage. Maybe some women and children would be saved. Maybe some people's emotional pains would be lessened, more tolerable or healed.

Men often say that there are not enough open lines of communication for them to express their concerns and their side of the picture. Men feel that everything is presented from a woman's point of view.

It would be great if more men would talk about their problems with medical personnel or support groups rather than hit their wives, girlfriends or children.

I would be happy if this book can help pave the way towards open lines of communication for everyone and can be of help in finding solutions.

Some people cannot cope with the stresses in their lives. It is true that a man who is in an altered state of mind, whether as the result of alcohol, drugs or a combination of both, does not realize his strength and can hurt a woman without intentionally trying. His strength during an Adrenaline rush in a fit of anger can turn deadly.

Did you know that even police officers are not extremely excited to receive domestic violence calls on their 911 lines? In too many cases, the police arrive, ready to arrest the abuser, only to find that the victim will not press charges on their abuser. The police get frustrated, understandably so. They are can't stop the abuse and what's worse, they know it will probably continue and maybe even get worse.

Please Stop The Presses For An Emergency Call

While this manuscript was at my Publisher I was overwhelmed with this emergency call and I asked them to stop the printing process. During this call I was informed that a friend, Vickie, was in a coma after her estranged husband allegedly got into her apartment in the early morning hours, rendered her defenseless in a horrible way and then hit her over the head with a baseball bat. He was arrested at the scene and the charges pending are for murder. God in his mercy could not leave such an incredible, beautiful, talented, mother of three in that comatose state so he called her to Heaven to take on another role. Vickie left behind wonderful memories and messages for all of us and there is tremendous sorrow among all of my friends and her family with her passing. Abuse is not about statistics. It is about real people's lives. It is also about what will happen to their children's lives. Whatever we can do to stop it is important. Please do what you can to help yourself and others and God Bless You.

There is no standard guide or map which will tell you exactly how to get out of a situation which is mentally, physically or emotionally abusive because each situation is unique. I encourage you to decide how you want to live your life; to visualize the lifestyle you want to create; take life one day at a time; seek positive support for your goals; eliminate negatives blocking your path; be flexible; and please consider issues of safety, money, legalities and emotional well-being. Of course, consider your children if you have any. Strive to think clearly and carefully about your plans and if you decide to leave a relationship or situation., ask for help if you need it and God Bless You.

29

FINALLY

Almost 10 years and 100 plus pages later, I am starting to believe that when you lose something, or more appropriately sometimes, when it is taken away from you, whether it's your job, a relationship, a business venture, or a significant amount of money earned in a certain way, it is probably because you are being forced to move on to something else because this thing is no longer serving your highest good or purpose in life.

It took many years to feel like I was not the victim in my losses and even longer to consider the notion that on some level, I had in advance chosen to have these experiences in this lifetime. What may disappear or end quickly can leave you contemplating the reason for its leaving or loss for many years, if not the rest of your life.

To look for the messages and lessons in my losses has lead to many interesting discoveries about myself and to this literary journey. I realize that by suffering emotional pain I have gained understanding and can be empathetic to those who experience similar heartaches or losses. I can try to help others heal.

Endings get us closer to new beginning, new possibilities. It's as if we're at the bus terminal of life where you know there's always another bus coming, yet one bus has to pull away from its spot for the next one to take its place.

I guess I've got to go now. My bus is coming.

RESOURCE GUIDE

As promised, here are some numbers to call for help or information in the United States.

NATIONAL DOMESTIC
ABUSE HOTLINE   1-800-799-SAFE

NATIONAL RESOURCE CENTER ON
DOMESTIC VIOLENCE 1-800-537-2238

BATTERED WOMEN'S
JUSTICE PROGRAM   1-800-903-0111

RESOURCE CENTER ON CHILD
PROTECTION AND CUSTODY 1-800-527-3223

ALABAMA   (205) 832-4842

ALASKA   (908) 272-1000
Alaska Network on Domestic Violence
and Sexual Assault   (907) 586-3650

Alaska Council on Domestic
Violence and Sexual Assault   (907)465-4356
P.O. Box 1112000, Juneau, Alaska 99811

ARIZONA   (602) 836-0858
Arizona Coalition Against Domestic Violence

ARKANSAS   (800) 332-4443
                                            (501) 376-3219

Arkansas Coalition Against Violence
To Women and Children   (501) 978-3600

CALIFORNIA
California Alliance Against
 Domestic Violence   (415) 457-2464

COLORADO
Colorado Domestic Violence Coalition   (303) 573-9023

CONNECTICUT
Connecticut Coaltion Against
Domestic Violence   (203) 524-5890

D.C.
D.C. Coalition Against Domestic Violence (202) 783-5332

FLORIDA
Florida Coalition Against
Domestic Violence   (904) 668-6862
Statewide   (800) 500-1119

GEORGIA
Georgia Advocates For Battered Women (404) 524-5959

HAWAII
Hawaii State Commission
on Family Violence   (808) 595-3900

ILLINOIS   (217) 789-2830
Statewide   (800) 603-HELP
                                         or (800) 603-4357

MICHIGAN
Michigan Coalition
Against Domestic Violence

(800) 99-NO-ABUSE
or (800) 996-6228
(517) 484-2924

MINNESOTA
Minnesota Coalition
For Battered Women

(612) 646-6177

MISSISSIPPI
Mississippi Coalition
 Against Domestic Violence

(601) 981-9146

MISSOURI
Missouri Coalition
Against Domestic Violence

(314) 634-4161

MONTANA
Montana Coalition
Against Domestic Violence

(800) 655-7867
(800) 655-7867

NEBRASKA
Nebraska Domestic Violence and
Sexual Assault Coalition

(402) 476-6256

NEVADA
Network Against Domestic Violence

(800) 992-5757
(702) 358-1171

NEW HAMPSHIRE
New Hampshire Coalition
Against Domestic Violence

(800) 852-3311
(603) 224-8893

NEW JERSEY
New Jersey Coalition For Battered Women (800) 572-7233
(609) 584-8107

NEW MEXICO
New Mexico State Coalition
Against Domestic Violence   (505) 246-9240

NEW YORK
New York Coalition Against
Domestic Violence   (800) 942-6906 English
(800) 942-6908 Spanish
(518) 432-4864

NORTH CAROLINA
North Carolina Coalition
Against Domestic Violence   (919) 956-9124

NORTH DAKOTA
North Dakota Coalition on
Abused Women's Services   (701) 255-6240

OHIO
Ohio Domestic Violence Network   (216) 651-8484

OKLAHOMA
Oklahoma Coaltion on Domestic
Violence and Sexual Assault   (800) 522-7233
(405) 557-1210

OREGON
Oregon Coalition Against Domestic
and Sexual Violence   (503) 239-4486

PENNSYLVANIA
Coaltion Against Domestic
Violence Services   (717) 545-6400
Eastern Pennsylvania   (800) 642-3150

RHODE ISLAND
Coalition Against Domestic Violence (401) 723-3051

SOUTH CAROLINA
South Carolina Coalition Against
Domestic Violence   (803) 254-3699

SOUTH DAKOTA
Coalition Against Domestic Violence
and Sexual Assault   (605) 225-5122

TENNESSEE
Task Force Against Domestic Violence (615) 386-9406

TEXAS
Texas Council on Family Violence (800) 876-4808
          (512) 794-1133
          (903) 793-Help

UTAH
Council on Domestic Violence   (801) 538-4100

VERMONT
Vermont Network Against
 Domestic Violence   (800) Abuse 95
       or (800) 228-7395
         (802) 223-1302

VIRGINIA
Virginians Against Domestic Violence (800) 838-8238
         (804) 221-0990

WASHINGTON
Washington Coalition Against
Domestic Violence   (800) 562-6025
                                               (206) 352-4029

WEST VIRGINIA
West Virginia Coalition Against
Domestic Violence   (800) 352-6513
                                               (304) 765-2250

WISCONSIN
Wisconsin Coalition On Domestic Violence (800) 333-7233
                                               (608) 255-0539
                                               (414) 832-1666

WYOMING
Wyoming Coalition Against Domestic Violence
And Sexual Assault   (307) 235-2814

The Internet

With the growth of computer usage, no Resource Guide would be complete without some mention of internet addresses which may be of interest. When looking up "Domestic Violence" and " Mental Abuse" and other related topics, there were literally hundreds of thousands of site addresses to search. These would fill a small library. This Resource

Guide is just a starting place. You will have to research on your own for more.

NATIONAL DOMESTIC VIOLENCE HOTLINE:
http://www.ndvh.org/
AMERICAN BAR ASSN. COMMISSION ON DOMESTIC VIOLENCE:

email: abacdv@abanet.org
You can also write to them at :
The American Bar Assn
Commission on Domestic Violence
740 15 st. NW 9th Flt
Washington, DC. 20005-1022

Please note that through the American Bar Assn. Commission on Domestic Violence information placed on the internet there is a potentially useful warning on the internet site that states that it may be possible for a computer saavy abuser to discover your internet activities. It gives some recommendations about how you can cover your tracks when doing this type of research and also states that a safer way to search for this type of information on the internet is to do the research at a local library, a friend's house or even through your job.

Other information found during my research that I'd like to pass to you:

Minnesota Center Against Violence and Abuse at the University of Minnesota
email: info@vaw.umn.edu

The Sounding Board Counseling Center
Listed as a comprehensive counseling and mental health facility specializing in domestic
violence, serving the whole US.
Crisis Line 1-800-829-1122

NOW AVAILABLE ON AUDIOCASSETTE OR CD:
To order "Without Me, You'll Be Eating Out of Garbage Cans" on audiocassette, send check or money order in US Dollars for $8.95 plus $2.50 s/h (Florida Residents please add appropriate sales tax) to the address below.

For this book on CD, please send check or money order in US Dollars for $12.95 plus $2.50 s/h (Florida Residents please add appropriate sales tax) to the address below.

Please allow up to six weeks delivery for all audiocassette or cd purchases.

Send payment in US Dollars to:
Lori Wilk
c/o Speak Up., Inc.
PO BOX 700264
St. Cloud, FL. 34770

For any questions email me at: loriwilk@hotmail.com

TO ORDER ADDITIONAL COPIES OF THIS BOOK
Please visit the Writer's Club Site on the Internet at:
http://www.books.writersclub.com
Then look under WC books and select "BUY THIS BOOK" and you will be guided through the order form.

Please visit the iUniverse.com book store at:
http://www.iUniverse.com/bookstore and search by the title.

For orders of large quantities, please contact the author.

   ***A percentage of the proceeds from the sale of this book, plus the sale of my audiocassettes and cds will be donated to organizations helping victims of abuse.

   Thank-you in advance for your help and support.

Disclaimer from the Author:

The information provided in this book was accurate at the time of publication to the best of my knowledge but is subject to change at any time without notice. Lori Wilk or Speak Up, Inc. Will not be responsible for any damages whatsoever arising out of, or in connection with the information contained herein, nor liable for any errors or omissions that may be found in such information nor do I guarantee, endorse or take responsibility for the results obtained through use of such information. You agree not to make any claims whatsoever against Lori Wilk or Speak Up, Inc. In connection with any of the information contained in this book.

For legal, medical or financial matters, it is advisable to seek professional help.

This book contains my opinions, take them, leave them or share them with anyone you think should read them. All decisions you make with your life are your own.

ABOUT THE AUTHOR

Lori Wilk is an award winning motivational speaker and television producer. She teaches business seminars throughout the US and makes appearances at groups and organizations.

To arrange a speaking engagement or special appearance, or to let me know what you think of my book, please write or send email.

Letters can be addressed to:
Lori Wilk
c/o Speak Up, Inc.
PO BOX 700264
St. Cloud, FL 34770

Email can be sent to:
loriwilk@hotmail.com